Challenges Facing Higher Education at the Millennium

Edited by
Werner Z. Hirsch
and
Luc E. Weber

AMERICAN COUNCIL ON EDUCATION ★
ORYX PRESS ★
Series on Higher Education
1999

The rare Arabian Oryx is believed to have inspired the myth of the unicorn. This desert antelope became virtually extinct in the early 1960s. At that time, several groups of international conservationists arranged to have nine animals sent to the Phoenix Zoo to be the nucleus of a captive breeding herd. Today, the Oryx population is over 1,000, and over 500 have been returned to the Middle East.

© 1999 by The American Council on Education and The Oryx Press
Published by The Oryx Press
4041 North Central at Indian School Road
Phoenix, Arizona 85012-3397

Published simultaneously in Canada
Printed and bound in the United States of America

♾ The paper used in this publication meets the minimum requirements of American National Standard for Information Science—Permanence of Paper for Printed Library Materials, ANSI Z39.48, 1984.

Library of Congress Cataloging-in-Publication Data

Challenges facing higher education at the millennium / edited by Werner Z. Hirsch and Luc E. Weber.
    p. cm. — (American Council on Education/Oryx Press series on higher education)
    Includes bibliographical references and index.
    ISBN 1-57356-293-9 (alk. paper)
    1. Education, Higher—Aims and objectives—United States. 2. Education, Higher—Aims and objectives—Europe. I. Hirsch, Werner Zvi, 1920–   . II. Weber, Luc. III. Series.
LA227.4.C514   1999
378—dc21   99-28204

To David Pierpont Gardner—
respected scholar,
distinguished university president,
creative philanthropic leader,
lifelong exemplar of the highest ideals in education—
his colleagues dedicate this book
with appreciation and admiration.

CONTENTS

PREFACE

I n Western Europe and North America, higher education, while highly valued and acclaimed by all, faces great challenges at the millennium. Therefore, the academic community and its leaders must take stock of its present status, explore the challenges of the future, and evaluate promising initiatives to meet these challenges. Recognition of these needs was the motivating force for the colloquium that convened at Glion, Switzerland, in May 1998.

Two fundamental views define the overall nature of the challenges. One view, held by David Saxon, president emeritus of the University of California, is that universities benefit greatly from stability and by and large can follow a deliberate evolutionary path in making adjustments in their academic enterprise. Unlike industry, which made major changes in virtually all its activities and in many cases has even reinvented itself, universities are too precious an institution to take risks in possibly following the wrong beacon.

A second view, which informed most of the discussion at the Glion Colloquium and is expressed in the papers of this volume, is much more activist. It considers higher education to be in need of taking major affirmative steps so that it can effectively pursue teaching and research and significantly contribute public service in a rapidly changing world.

Virtually all the papers in this volume reflect a sense of urgency in the light of commonly perceived crisis conditions. One reason is that significant parts of higher education have been rather static in a dynamic world. This assertion is especially valid in relation to teaching, which in most instances has not undergone a major change in the 50 years since the end of World War II. Until recently, use of blackboards and chalk has been common and teaching style has remained traditional. This state holds even for law schools, at a time when legal research has been computerized and has changed in important ways. While research in the physical and biological sciences in universities has made great strides, as it has in industry, greater efforts could be made to connect the university to industry, without compromising the integrity of the university.

Adjustments must be made, and it was in this spirit that the Glion Colloquium explored what promising initiatives higher education, and especially research universities, might creatively pursue. Underlying the Glion Colloquium's deliberations and papers is a view that the status and future of higher education is best explored by the following three sequential undertakings:

- Articulation of the values and academic mission of institutions of higher education
- Definition of credible scenarios of the general environment in which these institutions are likely to find themselves when seeking to fulfill their academic mission
- Development of initiatives to allow these institutions to achieve their mission

As to academic values, universities in Western Europe and North America have much in common. There is virtually universal agreement that a learning society is based on individual initiative assisted by the social, economic, and political environment provided by government. Within this setting, extension of human knowledge is largely based in academic institutions.

The mission of universities comprises a moral obligation to contribute to the intellectual, cultural, and economic betterment of society in general. For public universities, this is also a legal obligation, directed in part at the betterment of conditions in their country and region.

To meet this obligation, universities must strive to contribute to the discovery of new knowledge, and to instill an appreciation of the value of the pursuit of knowledge. In doing so, universities contribute to both the intellectual vitality and the economic well-being of society; produce educated citizens; train the next generation of leaders in the arts, sciences, and professions; and (particularly in the United States) actively engage in public service activities that bring faculty knowledge and research findings to the attention of citizens and industry.

Contributions to knowledge and to the economic well-being of society are accomplished chiefly at the graduate/professional level; production of educated citizens is accomplished chiefly at the undergraduate level; and production of future leaders of society, encouragement of productive interactions among persons of diverse backgrounds, and appreciation of the value of the pursuit of knowledge are accomplished at all levels. Provision of lifelong learning opportunities is also a major obligation.

Defining credible scenarios of the future educational environment involves a number of issues. They include large increases in the number of students to be educated; increasing demand for different forms of higher education and for institutions that will meet these demands; the use of new information technologies in teaching, research, and library services; the need to supply greater financial resources to support higher education; the evolution of new subjects for teaching and research; and the globalization and internationalization of higher education.

Finally, there is the challenge of identifying and perfecting future promising initiatives. In a narrow sense, these initiatives must increase the productivity of universities while preserving, and even extending, their level of excellence. Specific initiatives to improve productivity can have two positive aims—to expand the amount and quality of educational services provided without increasing cost, and to make the services provided more effective. The first strategy increases the size of the higher education pie; the second allows serving more students from a pie of a given size. The initiatives can be either internally or externally directed, either value laden or predominantly technological fixes.

A few examples of such initiatives include novel intellectual alliances within the university and new partnerships outside it; novel funding sources; new structures and flexible career paths; new patterns of governance, leadership, and management; distance learning; lifelong learning; and improved integration of teaching, research, and public service.

It was neither possible, nor even desirable, for a three-day colloquium to be all inclusive in the subjects covered. It had to be selective. Thus, the Glion Colloquium and this volume, except for its introductory chapter, focused on some key topics, each addressed by a distinguished leader in higher education. A brief overview of each chapter follows.

In the first paper of Part 1, "Missions and Values," Luc E. Weber uses a survey of all colloquium participants to present the major challenges facing higher education at the millennium. The two papers that follow examine education goals and values. David P. Gardner considers how higher education and its values evolved in the United States. In this connection, he offers his view of how American society and its values have undergone changes, particularly in the last 150 years. Paolo Blasi traces the history of European universities and their evolving values as articulated in the 1997 Association of European Universities statement on "The European Universities in 2010."

In Part 2, "The Effect of the Changing Environment on Higher Education," three papers examine the environment that higher education is likely to face in future years. James J. Duderstadt presents two sharply contrasting future environments confronting higher education, while Stanley O. Ikenberry focuses on the information revolution's likely impact on the university. Harold M. Williams examines the economics of higher education.

In Part 3, "Meeting the Challenge," a number of papers address specific initiatives. These initiatives can be grouped as addressing funding, alliance building, governance, and technology. Thus, Werner Z. Hirsch, recognizing the difficulty higher education faces in obtaining funding adequate for fulfilling its mission without raising tuition, explores a variety of unconventional funding sources. The following four papers focus on promising opportunities for forming alliances between institutions of higher education, especially research universities, and industry. Papers by Hans J. A. van Ginkel, Peter Preuss, and Dennis Tsichritzis probe ways for research universities to enter into mutually beneficial partnerships with industry and, at times, with government agencies. Heide Ziegler describes a novel venture of a new private university dedicated to working with industry in educating and training information scientists. Howard Newby undertakes the task of examining the many facets of the governance of higher education, a topic of such importance that the next colloquium will focus exclusively on it. Charles F. Kennel explores the challenging task of applying information technology to what is often considered the heart of any great university—its library. Finally, Alan Wagner offers insight into lifelong learning together with some empirical information.

While all the papers are future oriented, the three papers in Part 4, "The University of the Future," are particularly so. Jacob Nüesch takes aim at Western Europe, while Chang-Lin Tien and Frank H.T. Rhodes speculate mainly about the future of American higher education.

The Appendix reproduces the Glion Declaration—"The University at the Millennium"—which was issued immediately following the colloquium. In it, at the request of the members of the Glion Colloquium, Frank H.T. Rhodes gave expression to their collective views.

● ● ●

We thank the William and Flora Hewlett Foundation, the Swiss Science Agency, the Federal Institute of Technology in Zurich, the University of Geneva, the Swiss Rectors' Conference, the Geneva Academic Society, and Swissair for their generous financial support. We are also indebted to the Association of European Universities in Geneva, which kindly put Mrs. Mary O'Mahony, Deputy General Secretary, at our disposal for the full length of the Glion Colloquium.

Werner Z. Hirsch
University of California, Los Angeles

Luc E. Weber
University of Geneva

CONTRIBUTORS

Paolo Blasi has been rector of the University of Florence since 1991 and chairman of the Italian Rectors' Conference since 1994. A full professor of general physics since 1980, with intense research activity in the field of nuclear physics, Professor Blasi has been director of the Department of Physics of the University of Florence and has promoted and directed the realization of the European Laboratory of Non-Linear Spectroscopy and of the Center of Optronic Excellence based in Florence. He is also a member of the Administrative Board of the International Association of Universities (IAU) and a member of many advisory and administrative committees of Italian scientific and economic institutions. He has cooperated with the Italian Ministry of University and Scientific Research in drafting law proposals concerning higher education in Italy.

James J. Duderstadt is president emeritus and university professor of science and engineering at the University of Michigan. Before becoming president (1988-1996), he served at the University of Michigan as provost and vice-president for academic affairs (1986-1988), dean of the College of Engineering (1981-1986), and professor of nuclear engineering (1976-1981). He received his B.S. in engineering (with highest honors) from Yale University in 1964, his M.S. in engineering science from the California Institute of Technology in 1965, and his Ph.D. in engineering science and physics in 1967. Dr. Duderstadt was an Atomic Energy Commission (AEC) fellow from 1964 to 1968, and a recipient of the E.O. Lawrence Award from the U.S. Department of Energy in 1986. In 1991, he won the National Medal of Technology and was named National Engineer of the Year by the National Society of Professional Engineers (NSPE). He is a fellow of the American Nuclear Society, having won its Mark Mills Award in 1968 and its Arthur Holly Compton Award in 1985. He was chair of the National Science Board (1991-1994), and served on the National Academy of Engineering (NAE) Council and as a member of the American Physics Society and the American Academy of Arts and Sciences. He is currently director of the Millennium Project in Ann Arbor, Michigan.

David P. Gardner has served as president of The William and Flora Hewlett Foundation since 1993. Prior to that, he served as the tenth president of the University of Utah from 1973 to 1983 and as the fifteenth president of the University of California from 1983 to 1992. In 1981, the U.S. secretary of education appointed him chairman of the National Commission on Excellence in Education. The Commission's 1983 report, A Nation at Risk, sparked the national effort to improve and reform schooling in the United States. He is a fellow of the National Academy of Arts and Sciences and the National Academy of Public Administration and is a member of the National Academy of Education and the American Philosophical Society. Dr. Gardner has served on several national commissions concerned with American higher education and is a director of a number of private corporations and nonprofit institutions in the U.S.

Hans J.A. van Ginkel, a national from the Netherlands, became rector of the United Nations University (UNU) on September 1, 1997. From 1986 to 1997, he was rector of Utrecht University, which has some 25,000 students and at which some 350 Ph.D. theses are defended each year. Before becoming rector of Utrecht University, he served as dean of the Faculty of Geographical Sciences. As both an academic and university administrator, Dr. van Ginkel has been actively involved in inter-university development cooperation, in particular, with universities in Southern Africa, Central America, Guyana, and Indonesia. He holds many international offices, including the vice-presidency of the International Association of Universities (IAU). He served more recently as a member of the Steering Committee for the World Conference on Higher Education.

Werner Z. Hirsch is professor of economics at the University of California, Los Angeles, after having been at U.C. Berkeley, Washington University, Harvard University, and Cambridge University. He has been the founding director of public policy institutes at two universities. Dr. Hirsch has served on numerous boards, committees, and councils and in an advisory capacity to numerous federal, state, and local governments in the United States, as well as to international agencies and the RAND corporation. He received his B.S. in 1947 and his Ph.D. in 1949 from U.C. Berkeley. He is a member of Phi Beta Kappa and Sigma Xi and was awarded citations by the Senate of the State of

California and by the City of Los Angeles. He was also named by Japan's Zaisei-Gaku as a Kaizuito Hitobito "Scholar Who Helped Build the Field of Public Finance."

Stanley O. Ikenberry, former president of the University of Illinois, became the tenth president of the American Council on Education on November 1, 1996. Throughout his career, Dr. Ikenberry has been a national leader in higher education. He has chaired the boards of the Carnegie Foundation for the Advancement of Teaching, the National Association of State Universities and Land-Grant Colleges, the Association of American Universities, and the American Council on Education. Dr. Ikenberry served Pennsylvania State University as senior vice-president and as professor in the Penn State Center for the Study of Higher Education prior to assuming the Illinois presidency in 1979. Dr. Ikenberry received his B.A. at Shepherd College in Shepherdstown, West Virginia, in 1956. His M.A. and Ph.D. were awarded by Michigan State University in 1957 and 1960, respectively.

Charles F. Kennel has been director of the Scripps Institution of Oceanography since 1998. Prior to that, he served as executive vice-chancellor at UCLA (1996-1998), as associate administrator at NASA (1994-1996), and as professor of physics at UCLA (1967-1993). Professor Kennel received his A.B. from Harvard University in 1959 and his Ph.D. from Princeton University in 1964. He has been awarded the NASA Distinguished Service Medal, the Aurelio Peccei Prize by the Academia Lincei, the James Clerk Maxwell Prize by the American Physical Society, and the Hannes Alfven Prize by the European Geophysical Society. He was a faculty research lecturer at UCLA and is a member of the National Academy of Sciences and the International Academy of Astronautics.

Howard Newby took office as vice-chancellor of the University of Southampton in 1994, moving from the Economic and Social Research Council, where he was chairman and chief executive. He was formerly professor of sociology at the University of Essex and has held visiting appointments in Australia and the United States. From 1980 to 1983, he was professor of sociology and rural sociology at the University of Wisconsin, Madison. Professor Newby is currently a member of a number of government bodies concerned with the funding of research in the U.K. He is chairman of the Centre for the Exploitation of Science and Technology (CEST). He is vice-chair of the Committee of Vice-Chancellors and Principals (CVCP) and a member of the CVCP Executive Committee. He also serves on a number of CVCP steering and sector groups, and leads for the CVCP on European affairs.

Jacob Nüesch is former president of the Federal Institute of Technology in Zurich (1990-1997) and a current member of the International Committee of the Red Cross (ICRC). He was formerly the head of pharma research at Ciba Geigy in Basel, Switzerland, and an associate professor at the University of Basel, where he taught microbiology. He has done extensive research in applied microbiology and biotechnology, and has some 120 publications in these fields and in microbial biochemistry, molecular biology, and genetic engineering. Professor Nüesch has served as president of the Swiss Society of Microbiology and as secretary general of the Federation of European Microbiological Societies (FEMS). He received his Ph.D. in microbiology and phytopathology from the Federal Institute of Technology (ETH) in Zurich in 1960 and became a research scientist at Ciba AG in Basel in 1961. Dr. Nüesch has conducted extended research in biochemistry and molecular biology in Canada, the United States, and the Federal Republic of Germany.

Peter Preuss received his undergraduate degree from the Technical University of Hanover, Germany, in 1964. He was completing his doctorate in mathematics at the University of California, San Diego, when he founded one of the earliest software companies, specializing in the newly emerging field of computer graphics. He ran his company, Integrated Software Systems Corporation (ISSCO), for 17 years. It ultimately had over 500 employees, with 32 offices worldwide, and was traded on the NASDAQ. In 1985, Mr. Preuss founded the Preuss Foundation for Brain Tumor Research, specializing in facilitating communication among researchers. Since 1985, he has organized and run 28 highly specialized conferences for researchers in this field. Mr. Preuss was co-founder of the National Computer Graphics Association. He served a term on the Advisory Committee to the director of the National Institutes of Health and is a director of numerous for-profit and not-for-profit organizations. He is also a member of the California Council for Science and Technology and is currently serving a 12-year term on the Board of Regents of the University of California.

Frank H. T. Rhodes was president of Cornell University for 18 years before retiring in 1995, having previously served as vice-president for academic affairs at the University of Michigan. A geologist by training, Rhodes was a member of President Bush's Education Policy Advisory Committee. He has also served as chairman of the National Science Board and chairman of the boards of the American Council on Education, the American Association of Universities, and the Carnegie Foundation for the Advancement of Teaching. He was chairman of the American Council on Education's task force on minority education which produced the report *One-Third of a Nation* and for which former presidents Jimmy Carter and Gerald Ford served as honorary co-chairs. He holds over 30 honorary degrees. Rhodes has just completed a book on American universities. He is at present a member of the Washington Advisory Group.

Chang-Lin Tien holds the professorial title of NEC Distinguished Professor of Engineering, a post he assumed on July 1, 1997, after seven years' service as U.C. Berkeley's seventh chancellor—the first Asian-American to head a major research university in the United States. Concurrent with his chancellorship, he held the A. Martin Berlin Chair in mechanical engineering. A faculty member in Berkeley's Mechanical Engineering Department since 1959, he has been chair of the department (1974-1981) and vice-chancellor for research (1983-1985). He also served as executive vice-chancellor and UCI Distinguished Professor at the University of California, Irvine (1988-1990). Dr. Tien is internationally recognized for his scholarly contributions in the field of heat transfer. Born in Wuhan, China, and educated in Shanghai and Taiwan, Dr. Tien completed his undergraduate education at National Taiwan University. He came to the U.S. in 1956, and earned a master's degree and a Ph.D. at Princeton University in 1959. A recipient of numerous honorary doctoral degrees from universities in the U.S. and abroad, he currently serves on the boards of many institutions, including the Asia Foundation, Wells Fargo Bank, Raychem Corporation, Chevron Corporation, Air Touch Communications, and Kaiser Permanente.

Dennis Tsichritzis obtained his diploma from the Technical University of Athens in 1965 and his Ph.D. from Princeton University in 1968. He was for many years a professor of computer science at the University of Toronto. He participated in the launching of The University of Crete and founded the Research Institute for Computer Science in Crete. He is currently a professor at the University of Geneva. He has served since 1991 as chairman of the executive board of GMD, the German National Research Center for Information Technology. Professor Tsichritzis has worked in several areas of computer science, including theory, operating systems, database management systems, office automation, object-oriented systems, and multimedia systems. He is currently president of the European Research Consortium for Informatics and Mathematics (ERCIM), a member of the board of Real World Computing in Japan, a member of the board of the International Computer Science Institute in Berkeley, and chairman of Information Verbund Bonn Berlin.

Alan Wagner is principal administrator for the Directorate for Education, Employment, Labour and Social Affairs of the Organization for Economic Cooperation and Development. He was a member of the OECD team that coordinated a 12-country thematic review of the first years of tertiary education, and contributed to the preparation of the comparative report, *Redefining Tertiary Education* (OECD, 1999). An economist, he has written on tertiary education financing and internationalization. His comparative work at the OECD has included educational effectiveness reform and improvement, governance and management, and teachers and their education. Dr. Wagner received his A.B. (with distinction) from the University of Michigan and his M.A. and Ph.D. from the University of Illinois (all in economics). Prior to joining the OECD in 1988, he was research associate at the State University of New York at Albany and, previously, assistant professor at Purdue University.

Luc E. Weber was educated in the fields of economics and political science and has been professor of public economics at the University of Geneva since 1975. As an economist, he serves as an adviser to the federal and cantonal governments. He has also been a member of the Swiss Council of Economic Advisers for three years. Since 1982, Professor Weber has been strongly involved in university management and higher education policy in the capacities of vice-rector and then rector of the University of Geneva, as well as chairman of the Swiss Rectors' Conference. Presently, he is consul for international affairs of the latter, representing Swiss universities in three European higher education organizations. Professor Weber is a member of the board of the International Association of Universities and serves as an expert to various governmental and non-governmental organizations, such as the Association of European Universities, the Council of Europe, and the World Bank.

Harold M. Williams has practiced law and served as chairman of the board of a major American corporation. He was dean of the Graduate School of Management at UCLA, chairman of the U.S. Securities and Exchange Commission, and president and chief executive officer of the J. Paul Getty Trust. Professor Williams has also served as a regent of the University of California; as co-chairman of the California Citizens Commission on Higher Education; as a board member of the National Humanities Center; and on the Committee for Economic Development, the Council on Foreign Relations, and President Clinton's Committee on the Arts and Humanities.

Heide Ziegler is president of the private International University in Bruchsal, Germany, which she co-founded with her colleague Andreas Reuter in 1998. Between 1992 and 1996, she was president of the University of Stuttgart, after having been vice-president there for two years. She has been professor of English and American literature since 1984 and is director of the Stuttgart Seminar in Cultural Studies, which she founded in 1991. She earned her degrees in classics and English literature at the universities of Göttingen and Würzburg. Her publications center on Faulkner and postmodern American literature, and include a study on irony as a mode of consciousness in the contemporary American novel (1995).

PART 1

• • • • • • • • • • • • •

Missions and Values

CHAPTER 1

Survey of the Main Challenges
Facing Higher Education
at the Millennium

Luc E. Weber

T o make sure that the discussion would cover all the relevant issues for
the future of higher education, the participants in the Glion Colloquium were invited to submit in advance what they considered to be
the five main challenges facing higher education at the millennium, in particular for research universities. This introductory chapter to the collected
papers of the Glion Colloquium is a short commented survey of the participants' input, including my own.

Most of the issues raised in this summary are at the core of the following
chapters and are therefore developed at length there. But it is interesting to
note here that if nearly all the following contributions mention globalization,
new technologies, and the necessity to improve governance as the most
burning challenges, some issues considered as central in the replies to our
inquiry, such as the responsibility of universities towards society, the academic
profession, or student expectations, get relatively little attention in the main
contributions.

This result demonstrates that higher education policy and university management are extremely complex undertakings characterized by lots of vari-
ables and by sophisticated, and even diverse, relationships among the vari-
ables. Universities are certainly the most complex institutions humans have
ever conceived. They developed extremely slowly through the centuries, in
Europe mainly, to become by the golden 1960s in most countries of the world
(certainly in North America and generally in Europe) respected building
blocks of society, whatever their status, public or private. Although today,

universities educate a proportion of a class age up to 10 times larger than it was a century ago, their reputation is diminishing. They are increasingly criticized, mainly by politicians and private employers, and invited to change. Well-known management guru Peter Drucker (1997) goes so far as to say that "Thirty years from now the big university campuses will be relics. Universities won't survive."

In comparison with industries, and even with the state, universities have remained extremely conservative institutions. It is therefore not surprising that all participants in the Glion Colloquium are convinced that universities have to change. Some believe that an incremental change process will do; others assert that change must be revolutionary; but no one believes in simplistic solutions drawn from the experience of industry management, as is often proposed during public discussion.

The key issues raised in response to our inquiry among the participants in the colloquium, and often developed in their own contributions, are rather diverse. The majority of them can be considered as traditional, aiming at improving the way research universities are fulfilling their different missions and governing themselves. However, some are clearly of a more revolutionary nature, announcing the end of traditional research universities if they do not adapt rapidly to the globalization of the world and do not take sufficiently into account the impact new technologies will have on the dissemination of knowledge. All admit that the future of research universities is less bright than their past, and even bleak, if universities do not reengineer themselves internally as well as rapidly reposition themselves within society.

The main challenges as perceived by the participants in the colloquium can be summarized under the seven following headings, the last one focusing on the main similarities and differences between the United States and Western Europe:

1. The changing environment
2. Missions
3. Students and teaching
4. The academic profession
5. Higher education finance
6. Governance
7. Comparison between the United States and Western Europe

THE CHANGING ENVIRONMENT

It is at least implicit in each contribution to this volume that accelerating geopolitical, economic, and technological changes, which affect the whole world, do not spare the university. Even if in their secular history, in particular in the Old World, the universities had to face difficult periods, now, for the first time ever, the way in which they fulfil their missions or even their existence is challenged not only by political threats, but also by technological and economic changes and pressures. First, the corporate world has had to change; now it is the turn of higher education. In particular, two strong forces are at work—globalization (or internationalization) and the information technology revolution.

Globalization

Globalization and, in particular, the rapid growth and development of the "knowledge industry"—the quantity of knowledge seems to double every five years—will profoundly change the educational system as the ability to move information more quickly and economically becomes greater and more widespread. These developments will require a repositioning of the university. Because universities have traditionally dispensed courses only regionally to their students, they have benefited from a regional monopoly. However, as we know from experience, monopolies based on regional proximity cannot survive the globalization movement. Therefore, universities will experience competition, worldwide and regionally. For some, it is a threat, but for others, it is a new opportunity offering universities the possibility to go beyond their regional role.

To act globally and in a competitive environment, the university, whether it likes it or not, must consider students to be clients by adapting programs to students' needs and wishes. Teaching, and even research, can no longer be decided essentially by the teachers and researchers, but should take much more into account the specific wishes of the students, as well as the needs of different types of students. In particular, most participants believe that universities should aggressively enter the field of lifelong learning because the accelerating obsolescence of knowledge and the changing needs of the labor market are increasing demand in this area. Moreover, one European participant, who is not a native English speaker, believes that English should become the predominant language in higher education, as it already is for research, a change that does not preclude the necessity to preserve a cultural heritage, of which the native language is a key element.

The Influence of Technology

Most participants note that the exploding information and telecommunication technologies offer new potential for producing and distributing knowledge. Teleteaching, in one way or another, is gaining ground. Part of a course can be imported via networks and combined with local content, which brings in international expertise. On the other hand, networks offer the chance to export courses and to amortize their costs on a large number of students.

Distance learning is also made possible at a high level because courses can be delivered directly to the student's desk through the Internet or on cheap CDs and DVDs. However, these digital courses are expensive to develop; therefore, universities must decide in which fields they want to build or keep up their international visibility and in which they can rely on imported contributions. Moreover, they will have more than ever to constitute networks to develop such programs.

MISSIONS

Responsive and Responsible Universities

Most participants seem to accept, without saying it explicitly, that the three fundamental missions of universities—teaching, research, and community service—are fundamentally correct, but argue that these should be taken more seriously. On one hand, universities should listen more carefully to society to learn and understand its changing needs and expectations, as well as its perception of higher education, especially in light of the forces driving change. Universities should be more responsive to needs when offering new study programs or starting new research. They should also show a greater willingness, or even take the lead in cooperating with industry, the state, and other higher education institutions. Universities and their units should be reliable partners for companies, institutions, and all other partners in society.

On the other hand, universities should sharpen their sense of responsibility towards society. More than ever, they are the only independent tenants of collective values and culture and the best placed to express constructive criticism and to suggest new ideas. They have been able to play this role more or less freely for centuries. This responsibility is as important in the present globalized world dominated by the power of the market and shortsighted politicians, as it was in periods of obscurantism or totalitarian regimes. The greatest threat is that knowledge, which is traditionally a public good available to all those seeking it, might become a private good reserved only for those who can pay for it.

The corollary of that search for more responsiveness and a greater sense of responsibility is greater transparency and accountability. The high cost of higher education and research is a heavy burden on society at large, whoever pays most, whether the state or individuals. Therefore, universities should not, as they were too long inclined to do, pretend that they are above the crowd and not accountable to anyone. Universities, public or private, belong to society and therefore have to be both transparent and accountable. This need implies more humility and internal democracy, as well as a greater effort at communication.

Among the concrete proposals made by the colloquium participants to improve the ways in which universities fulfil their missions, the following actions are the most relevant:

- Open up to the new public knocking at the door by responding to the sophisticated needs of adults in the workplace while providing broader lifetime learning opportunities for all in society.
- Participate with industry in the improvement of technology transfer from basic research to the marketing of new products.
- Develop among the student community greater sensitivity towards sustainable development.
- Educate students to be not only good "technicians" in their disciplines, but also good citizens, able to understand and criticize the development of society in a constructive way.

The Changing Shape of Research Universities

The second main issue raised about the missions of universities is their shape and fundamental culture. In particular, some participants in the colloquium believe that the two main characteristics of the research university are at risk. First, the increasing sophistication of advanced research, as well as the need to improve the quality of teaching programs, are creating a deepening gap between research activities and teaching activities, at least at the graduate level. Research will more and more be done in specialized institutions, publicly or privately funded, and undergraduate teaching will be offered by establishments that develop a superior pedagogical culture. Research universities may limit themselves to educating young researchers. For the Europeans attached to the Humboltian model, which pleads for the full integration of teaching and research under the same roof, this would mean the end of the university.

Increasing competition and transparency, as well as the resulting search for quality, will also threaten the model of the comprehensive university. Acting in a more competitive and transparent market for innovation and knowledge transfer, the universities will lose their best potential customers if they cannot assure high quality standards. This trend will force the most ambitious institutions to concentrate their resources in the disciplines where they are good, or where they would like to be good, and possibly to create networks or even to merge with other complementary institutions. Traditionally realized at the level of a region, such concentrations will be increasingly done across national borders or even on a worldwide scale, all the more so since new communication technologies can be integrated into the teaching and research processes.

Emergence of Competitors to Traditional Universities

Many participants see that the new world is bringing with it the emergence of new educational providers (e.g., for-profit institutions, mega-universities, and information "brokers" of distance learning such as the Western Governors University (WGU) in the U.S. or Ariane in Europe), as well as a tendency to commercialize research results to increase the income stream for research. This tendency has certain positive aspects. Apart from diverting additional money to teaching and research and broadening the output capacity of the higher education sector, it can introduce in the system establishments that may be more efficient and in particular more capable of responding to current needs.

However, it does introduce an important element of insecurity into the higher education system. The best education institutions run along with the worst. This situation requires quality assessment for the sake of protecting consumers, but also assessment of the quality of teaching and learning for those organizations using new pedagogical means.

Regarding the commercialization of research, the pertinent issue is the well-known problem of safeguarding the independence of the researcher, with respect to the choice of the research subject, the honesty of his or her findings, and the publication and exploitation of the results.

Finally, the emergence of a greater separation between teaching and research will slowly blur the distinction between universities and colleges, or more generally between undergraduate education within research universities and professional vocational training offered in higher education non-university organizations like technical higher schools or *Fachhochschulen* in the German-speaking part of Europe.

STUDENTS AND TEACHING

Nearly all participants state that the teaching mission of the university, as well as the response to student expectations of higher education, will have to gain in importance in the university of the future.

Students

When looking specifically at students, access to higher education is the dominating theme. Higher education in North America and in Western Europe is in a more or less advanced process of massification. The growing demand for higher education has its origins not only in social aspiration but is justified by the increased requirements of the labor market, being caused by the application of increased knowledge. Apart from the capacity of absorption of higher education institutions, which is mainly a financial and possibly a political issue, the main problem is access to higher education. In this respect, our societies have not yet succeeded in promoting equal access independent of social origin. They have still to promote that social requirement. This objective, although broadly accepted, appears more difficult to reach as the new financial developments, in particular increased student fees, substitution of loans for grants, and diminishing subsidies to student facilities, increase the problem. This situation seems to be more serious in the United States where even the middle class is beginning to feel the pressure.

Teaching

The other side of the coin, teaching, raises questions that are even more crucial. First, the knowledge society requires people who are well educated more than people who are specifically trained; to satisfy demand, universities should organize their teaching programs on a broader scale. The consequence should be to consider education as a continuing process, which will not stop after university. The knowledge society, which exposes young people to more new information in a year than their grandparents encountered in a lifetime, makes illusory the ability to transmit enough knowledge through the process of teaching. Participants believe that the capacity to learn has become crucial. Therefore, the whole traditional process of teaching has to be transformed. This implies the use of all adequate pedagogical supports and that the role of the teacher is becoming that of an animator. This is a great change that many teachers will have difficulty making. This change of paradigm will also make it more difficult to assess quality because it will be necessary to assess not only the quality of teaching, but also the quality of learning, which means assessing the performance of graduates in the world of work! Is this feasible?

The other key word when discussing teaching is "internationalization." In a global world, the possibility for a student to study part of the curriculum at another university is not only beneficial in terms of general culture, but may also allow a broadening of the field of specialization. However, to make mobility feasible, it is essential to assure mutual recognition of degrees and credit points, while at the same time allowing for individuality and diversity.

THE ACADEMIC PROFESSION

The faculty and all other teachers and researchers are by far the greatest resource of a university. They are those who know best the discipline, even broadly defined. The best-organized university is worth nothing if it cannot count on a qualified teaching staff; an unqualified staff means poor teaching and unimaginative research. This is why university departments and university leaders should pay great attention not only to the selection of people but also to the management of this rare human resource. Our inquiry about key challenges has shown that three difficult questions must be answered—the changing role of teachers, the position of tenure, and the provision of a new generation of staff to fill vacant positions.

The Changing Role of Teachers

Teachers will have to accept that their role is changing; they will be decreasingly information providers and increasingly animators and commentators in charge of giving context and in-depth understanding of an area. Moreover, as is already the case for research, they will be confronted with growing competition in their teaching assignments thanks to increasing transparency on the type and quality of courses available elsewhere and through multimedia.

University leaders complain regularly that faculty are more faithful to their discipline than to their university. Faculty are also criticized for not being sensitive to the needs and perceptions of the community that they are supposed to serve, as well as for having a shortsighted vision about the changing needs and expectations of society. This is a sensitive point because the support of a community for its university depends greatly on the conviction that the institution cares. As one participant phrased it, "teachers should not only be responsible for themselves, but also co-responsible for their institution as a whole."

Finally, the conflict between high specialization in one discipline and multi-disciplinarity should receive more attention. Traditionally, a researcher gets academic recognition for publishing specialized papers in one discipline, whereas participating in multi-disciplinary research groups requires patience, and the visibility of output is low because results are shared and are not at the frontier of knowledge in one specific discipline. Considering that multi-disciplinarity is crucial to better serve the community, faculty and researchers should be induced, or even compelled, to participate in multi-disciplinary projects.

The different issues mentioned above raise the question of the employment contract and even of the limits to academic freedom. It appears to many participants that to improve the coherence and therefore the quality of the teaching programs and to make the institution more helpful to the community, the employment contract and individual academic freedom should be redefined. Faculty should perhaps be statutorily obliged to give part of their time to serve community or societal needs and should enjoy total academic freedom only if it is consistent with the objectives of the department or institution.

Tenure

Tenure is another crucial and difficult issue. The rapidly changing world, the unprecedented speed at which knowledge is created, and economic pressures are causing university institutions to place greater emphasis on flexibility.

They must concentrate resources on some selected fields at the expense of others, a need that implies closing departments or hiring more non-tenured track faculty. Moreover, some senior faculty are perceived as no longer productive. Given these and other considerations, a few participants believe that tenure should be redefined. More precisely, tenure should be subordinated to some more restrictive conditions than those prevailing today; it should be easier to cancel tenure when a department is shut down or if the quality evaluation of teaching and research is insufficient. However, at the same time, measures should be taken to offer alternative solutions for those losing tenure, like offering alternative occupation within or outside the institution or introducing a flexible age-of-retirement scheme. However, limitation to tenure should be handled carefully to prevent discouraging young researchers from investing the necessary time in research to pursue an academic career.

Developing a New Generation of Staff

The extraordinary development of the university sector in the 1960s and 1970s brought an equivalent increase in the number of teaching staff. Twenty to thirty years later, those appointed at that time have to be replaced. This need for replacements poses not only a quantitative problem of finding quality successors, but the situation also creates an extraordinary opportunity to adapt the university supply to the changing social demand and to enhance university responsibility towards society. This is also an occasion to weight selection criteria differently, to take into account the changing role of teachers in a world of lifelong learning and quasi unlimited access to information, and to stress more the pedagogical quality and the entrepreneurial aptitude of the candidates. Postgraduate education should also be adapted to new requirements.

HIGHER EDUCATION FINANCE

The financing of universities is becoming increasingly difficult for the following three reasons:

- The public sector is hard pressed with tasks mainly on the transfer side of the budget (e.g., attending to an aging population, health care, poverty, and foreign aid), as well as with security issues and the maintenance of public infrastructure. Consequently, the percentage share of the revenues being devoted to higher education is bound to diminish.

- The private sector is less and less ready to transfer money to universities without getting a service in return or without being able to influence their activities.
- The cost of providing university education and of doing research continues to grow significantly more than increases in the cost of living.

Therefore, institutions are seriously challenged to take measures on both sides of the budget, that is, to secure or even increase their revenues as well as to decrease their unit costs of creating new knowledge and transmitting it. Any institution missing these points will inevitably decrease in scope and quality.

Securing Revenue

One of the most important issues, because its consequences are socially far-reaching, is to determine to what extent education and research are a public or a private good. The response to this question is partly factual (in general terms, basic research is essentially public, education of traditional students is partly private and partly public, and lifelong learning and applied research are predominantly private), but there is a high margin for political interpretation. Moreover, it would be important to know more about the distributional effects of different financing schemes and the exact burden borne by each generation.

In any case, there is a clear tendency towards a greater diversification (differentiation) of income sources within the state (different departments or levels of government) and within the private sector (student fees, capital endowment, commercialization of services, loans at a privileged interest rate, or grants from charity organizations). However, again, a necessary condition for a successful income campaign—aimed at either the public or the private sector—is more transparency and more accountability on the part of the institution.

Reducing Costs

On the expenditure side, two types of measures should be used more intensively. First, higher education institutions have been, in general, very bad at fixing clear priorities. Now, one cheap but extremely difficult way to finance new priority projects is to save money in sectors whose value to the university and to society has greatly diminished; in other words, universities should not necessarily always try to expand, but should more seriously consider renewing themselves through reallocating resources. However, such a more dynamic policy requires not only vision and courage, but also an organizational structure and a process for taking and implementing unpopular decisions.

Secondly, higher education institutions should much more energetically embrace their production or cost function. Teaching and research are labor intensive and therefore their unit costs tend to increase more rapidly than the cost of living, with the consequence that they permanently need more money to produce a given level of service. However, it seems presently possible to stabilize this tendency or even to reverse it. The new technologies, even if they require huge initial investments, allow universities to spread part of the cost of teaching over a large number of students all over the world so that the unit cost of teaching many courses could be decreased. Regarding research, there is also potential for saving in using, for example, simulation methods instead of full laboratory experiences. However, we have to be aware that the use of new technology to decrease costs implies a much closer cooperation between different institutions, which requires networking or merging of operations.

Moreover, many participants expect that private corporations strongly involved in computer, publishing, or entertainment businesses will take an increasing part of the share of this market for teaching and research tools. Opinions differ as to what extent this foreseeable development is a threat or a chance for traditional universities. Experience has shown that the publication of books has been a strong support to teaching and that members of the university community have been by far the main providers of content. Although the same can happen with the production of any sort of digitized courseware, there is one great difference—the production of new courseware requires a collective effort on the part of many teachers and the participation of specialists in the use of sophisticated equipment. This requires universities to network and form alliances with private firms.

GOVERNANCE

The governance of higher education institutions and particularly of research universities is probably the most important as well as the most complex issue in higher education policy. In a world of rapid change and stagnant or diminishing resources, a university cannot simply be administered, but must be governed so that it continually adapts to the new scientific and societal environment without neglecting its responsibility. The current practice of shared governance, which is deeply embedded in North American and Western European universities, worked well in a phase of stable circumstances or in a time of increasing resources, but has visible shortcomings in times of stress or constraint, as well as in times of rapid change. Overcoming these shortcomings is the main challenge facing higher education nowadays.

Main Shortcomings

The decision structure of traditional universities is slow and cumbersome. It is based on a faculty/department structure, and decisions are taken via many internal committees. Decisions typically require consensus among the faculty members. This structure hinders the decision process and leads to extremely slow reaction. The very nature of the process inhibits and impairs the ability of leadership to lead, therefore contributing to the perpetuation of an obsolete past.

Ways to Improve University Governance

The participants unanimously believe that if universities want to remain essential players in tomorrow's world of knowledge, they can hardly camp on traditional positions and hope for better days. They are expected to change, and they have to do it by themselves. Therefore, they have to restructure themselves to be able to do more with less.

Strong leadership is needed. However, what is leadership in a university where the wealth of knowledge and creative potential is, as in no other human organization, at the base of the pyramid (faculty, postgraduate, and advanced graduate students)? Does leadership mean that there should be one strong person who should decide on budgets, on infrastructure, and on cost, and who should be able to reposition and redeploy staff according to requirements or who would even decide on each unit's strategic positioning? Such leadership would mean that the "boss" knows better than the other actors what is good for the development of each unit and is able to impose decisions onto the university community. Applicable for a small and specialized institution, this "single" manager model is hardly feasible in a university.

Better leadership in such an organization has to combine the traditions of academic freedom and collective decision making with the new requirements outlined above, that is, the necessity to make and implement important and often unpopular decisions in a timely manner. Leadership in a university will still rely on shared governance, but, the balance of power between the university administration and the faculty must be shifted in favor of leaders so that the dominant conservative process of present systems makes room for a more progressive process.

The conception of this broad-based leadership model is particularly challenging and should therefore receive first priority in the agenda of university leaders. The study of the vast and diverse experience accumulated in the universities of different countries can be helpful. Most of the main ways to improve university leadership will address the following points:

- Organize the university as a federation or as a holding company and apply the principle of subsidiarity; in other words, give as much autonomy as possible to the different units to allocate human and financial resources as they wish.
- Eliminate multi-layered decision processes; only one level has to be competent, and the level above is responsible for controlling.

- Give real competence for final decisions to the president/rector for such crucial questions as budget and strategic plan, infrastructure, and allocation of human resources (faculty); the community must become accustomed to stronger management.
- Set aside a special budget to allow the management of the institution to promote new programs through financial incentives and to cover the costs of closing an activity that is no longer a priority.
- Develop university policy by elaborating a strategic plan that involves the whole community; the final decision has to be taken by the president/rector, and the plan has to be implemented according to competencies at different levels.
- Increase the level of management skills of the leaders at the different organizational levels, including board members, if any.

The reengineering of the decision process will also mean adapting the structure of the organization. However, because structure varies enormously from country to country and even from institution to institution in a single country, we cannot comment on that here.

Finally, and this is particularly true for higher education institutions funded mainly by the state, wide and real autonomy should be granted to them. To run a university is an extremely complex task; shortsighted political intervention can only do harm. The institution as a whole should have a clear mission that defines what is expected from it, should be free to act, and should be accountable. In addition, this autonomy should not only be enshrined in a general law, but also respected in all fields of legislation.

COMPARING THE UNITED STATES AND WESTERN EUROPE

We have identified and described the main challenges facing higher education without mentioning any differences between the United States and Western Europe. Is there really such similarity in the development of the two regions? The answer to this question is mixed and made difficult because Europe itself is much diversified. In brief, we observe that the main differences lie more in the original institutional setting or historical heritage and stage of development than in different challenges facing the two regions.

This is not the place to examine in detail institutional differences. The most important one is that private universities are common in the U.S. and an exception in Europe. To some extent, the same is true for boards of trustees or regents. The search for sponsors to finance the construction of university buildings or to fund research and study programs is part of daily life in the U.S. but is just beginning in Europe. For that reason, the role of the president/rector is somehow different, with the American president spending a greater part of his or her time in lobbying potential sponsors than the European one.

If the level of recognition of the intellectual autonomy of universities is high—although not absolute—in both regions, the administration of American universities is apparently less constrained by public rules or direct political intervention. Moreover, tuition fees cover a much greater share of the budget in the United States than in Europe. Finally, the organization of the higher education sector is different. In the United States, one huge sector integrates top-quality research universities as well as a great number of teaching colleges and even of two-year colleges. The American system offers top-level academic education, as well as focused vocational training or even general education as provided in the last years of high school in Europe. The European higher education system, although partly different from one country to another, is in general stratified in two different sets of institutions pursuing similar missions and aims: on one side, the universities, which have not been qualified as "research universities" because they promote research by definition and, on the other side, high vocational training institutions.

Although these institutional differences are important, we believe that the challenges facing universities on both sides of the Atlantic are similar. The most visible differences, if any, are in how these challenges are met. Clearly, the most striking changes in their environment are the same: the explosion of knowledge and the revolution in information technology; the emergence of new players; the new public, in particular for lifelong learning; tight budgets; the need for greater transparency and accountability; and the threat of increasing intervention from the state, the sponsors, or the governing boards.

The crucial question for universities on either side of the Atlantic is therefore their capacity to be responsive to this new environment without abandoning their responsibility towards society. This question is mainly one of organizational structure and governance to adapt the institution to new realities, as well as a question of ability to convince the main sponsors—public or private—that universities are worth supporting in the long run.

CONCLUSION

This survey of the most burning issues facing higher education, and in particular research universities, as identified by the participants in the Glion Colloquium, demonstrates clearly that universities are facing great challenges at the millennium. Even if the issues raised by participants vary, opinion is converging with respect to the main trends and challenges. Each participant has at least implicitly mentioned that globalization and internationalization, as well as the information technology revolution are pushing universities into a competitive market for higher education and research, and that the combination of decreasing support on the part of the state or sponsors and increasing costs will force universities to take unpopular measures to do more for less.

Clearly, universities will have to adapt more rapidly to this changing environment to keep the unique position they have been able to build through the ages and to assume their responsibility as guarantor of societal value and inherited culture.

As to solutions, three main areas of action are proposed: adapt the academic profession, improve the financial situation by making an effort on the income as well as on the expenditure side of the budget, and reform governance. The main divergence of opinion lies not in the differences between the American and the Western European situation, but in the evaluation of the importance of the threats to traditional universities and therefore in the scope of the measures to be taken to maintain or even improve the high profile universities once had. Some believe radical measures are an obligation to help universities from falling into mediocrity and being replaced by well-organized profit-seeking institutions. Others, also convinced of the necessity for change, believe that a well-designed adaptation process will be adequate. The reality will depend mainly on the still unknown speed at which new technologies will penetrate large layers of the population.

Although this survey does not pretend to be exhaustive, the most relevant issues have certainly been mentioned. Most of these issues are more extensively developed in the individual contributions that follow.

REFERENCE

Drucker, P. F. (1997). Interview: "Seeing Things as They Really Are," *Forbes, 159,* pp. 122–28.

CHAPTER 2

Meeting the Challenges of the New Millennium

The University's Role

David P. Gardner

During the last half of the nineteenth century, much of the higher learning in the United States was reshaped in response to a rapidly growing, expanding, and changing nation. American education accomplished this reshaping by holding on to the best of the past—the liberal arts college modeled on the British undergraduate experience—borrowing the best of the new from continental Europe—the German emphasis on empiricism, research, and graduate study—and adding ideas of their own—the land-grant concept embodied in the Morrill Act of 1862, which increased student access, reconfigured and broadened both the curriculum and public service, and laid the foundation for the country's great public universities. Thus was formed the modern American university.

As the following examples show, the winds of change are again blowing hard, but this time in a more diverse country and in a far more volatile and interdependent world.

- Ideological commitments that had locked in communist governments for decades are giving way, sometimes chaotically and certainly unevenly, to greater political openness, increased international trade, widespread economic development, the aggressive use of new technologies, free market principles, and more democratic institutions and practices.
- The past two decades have seen the emergence of the Pacific Rim as a potent force in the world's economy, temporary setbacks notwith-

standing. The rise of Japan and the newly industrialized states of Asia has challenged assumptions about American dominance of the global marketplace, our current successes aside, as will the impending economic and monetary integration of Western Europe.

- East and West are today struggling less with each other than they are struggling in common with the forces of modernity—the technological revolution, modern science, the industrialization of labor, and large-scale urbanization. These forces are changing the world not just at the margin but at the core.

- Ideas blow across political boundaries, even into the most insulated of nations and societies—disquieting, troubling, indeed, in some instances, overturning even the most ideological and inflexible of established orders, as occurred in the former Soviet Union.

All these forces—economic, political, ideological, religious, social, and cultural—are interrelated and global in their significance and effect; they are abetted by a revolution in telecommunications, commercial air travel, student and faculty exchanges across national boundaries, satellites, and the computer. The leading nations in this dramatically altered economic and political environment will be those with surplus capital, national self-discipline, advanced technology, and superior education. In respect to this agenda for the future, the United States has both advantages and disadvantages as it struggles to define its role and place in this changing world scene. The list of American problems will sound familiar.

- The growing gap between the country's rich and poor and an ominous growth in the underclass—the unemployable poor caught in a vicious cycle of drugs, alienation, broken families, and crime, especially in the inner cities.

- The erosion of our sense of community and civil life, and the corresponding diminishment of local governments as power and authority shift to state and federal authorities.

- The nation's troubled system of public schools, chronically underfunded and underperforming compared with many, if not most, of the world's advanced industrial countries.

- The disquietude within the body politic, in spite of a booming economy, attributable partly to the problems just mentioned, partly to the knowledge that the U.S is a less dominant player on the world scene, and partly, at least in the western and southwestern states, to large-scale in-migration from Mexico, Latin America, and Asia, which is reshaping the ethnic and racial balance within American social, political, and economic systems, and straining society's assimilative capacities.

On the other hand, the U.S. also has some striking advantages.

- The nation possesses remarkably stable political, social, and economic systems and fosters a society that not only adapts to change but actually encourages it. The American openness to new ways of doing things is a tremendous advantage in a world characterized by constant technological change, as is the nation's willingness to accept new talent and fresh ideas from throughout the world.
- The best American universities, with a handful of notable exceptions, are the finest in the world. The vigor of basic research enterprise in the U.S. is truly exceptional, and its democratic and open spirit helps ensure that the best flourish. Americans continue to capture most of the Nobel Prizes year after year, surely an indication that Americans are doing something right—or at least did so within the professional lifetime of the recipients.
- The creativity and productivity of American business also count for what is right in the country. Much is made these days of the short-term focus of American companies—too much, in my opinion, because that view fails to take into account the extent to which American companies have recognized their problems and have restructured during the 1980s and 1990s. Business has been more strategic and energetic in responding to change than have either the universities or government as the positive corporate bottom line today makes clear.
- The U.S. dollar is valued not only because of its comparative stability and strength in world currency markets but also because it is the currency of a society with an enormous capacity for adaptability, hard work, creativity, and an open attitude and a positive response toward change.

For the world generally, the most essential challenges in the coming years will be to deal with the diminishing sovereignty of nations, the growing balkanization of countries and societies, the increasing gap in wealth between developed and underdeveloped countries, the relentless growth of world population, the mass migration of peoples, the rising level of religious fundamentalism, gross environmental degradation, shrinking stocks of basic food supplies relative to need, including water, and the education of the young for the world they will live in—not for the one with which we are familiar now.

The Western university, especially in the United States and unevenly elsewhere, has a vital role to play and a nearly unique capability to help with these problems because most of them will require knowledge, brainpower, skilled intelligence, and judgement to solve, or at least to manage. The university, of all institutions, has the capacity to help define these issues, to analyze and examine them, to discuss creative ways of coping with them, and to share this knowledge and these insights not only with the young but also with the larger society. The university is also able to do so with less ideological or political bias and with more impartiality and objectivity than any other institution, public or private. Moreover, the university is the principal repository of educated and trained personnel, of the sophisticated tools and intellectual resources needed to do the work, and of the infrastructure critical to the task. It is *the* institution with sufficient experience, independence, and authority to carry out its work while possessing a credible reputation in the larger society.

In coming years, the university should be more central to efforts to comprehend and cope with these forces for change. The university, more than any other collective and credible enterprise in our society, should be playing the key role. The question, of course, is: Will it? The answer: Well, probably, but not inevitably.

ADVERSE TRENDS IN AMERICAN HIGHER EDUCATION

If not deflected or checked, a number of adverse trends in the United States, could compromise or diminish the university's capacity to play its distinctive and natural role in this changing world.

Public Funding

The funding of public higher education nearly everywhere in the U.S. ebbs and flows with the times—with changing public attitudes towards government, taxes, and the universities themselves, and with the public's assessment of the universities' work and worth. And the universities have in the 1990s lost heavily on all counts, just as they did in the mid- to late-1960s, but today for fundamentally different reasons.

More than 30 years ago, the Free Speech Movement at Berkeley, general student unrest throughout the universities of Western Europe and the United States, and violent and widespread student demonstrations in the U.S. against the war in Vietnam led to dramatically reduced public support and respect for universities. This loss of respect damaged them, nearly irreversibly, for almost two decades. The mid- to late-1980s, however, were a period of healing and renewed support for universities from both the public and private sectors. The early to mid-1990s, in contrast, were financially hurtful to these institutions (nearly as severe in some instances as were the years of the Great Depression in the 1930s). Moreover, the universities were disproportionately hurt when compared with virtually every other aspect of publicly funded activities. The universities' position was weakened vis-à-vis growing public support and relatively better funding for schools, health, welfare, and prisons. It now appears that the loss of funding, unlike following the years of student unrest, will not be redressed even though significant increases in enrollment are imminent in many states and levels of tuitions and fees have reached historic highs.

The universities' response to these fiscal problems was to seek operational efficiencies, reduce services, erode student/faculty ratios, defer plant and equipment maintenance, reduce administrative staff, and increase tuitions and fees charged to students. These and other measures used over the years to deal with such fiscal stringencies were always thought to be more temporary than permanent. Today, they have become permanent, and the universities' response will now need to be concerned less with efficiency and more with purpose and pedagogy.

Governmental policies tend to abet, indeed, sometimes to mandate, such university responses through budgetary language and statutes or regulations enacted or promulgated to induce compliance. Examples are mandated levels of staffing; tuitions and fees; enrollment levels; staff and faculty compensation; space standards; and so forth. Such governmental mandates are not always unwelcomed by academic administrators and governing boards, especially during times of fiscal exigencies when they enable university authorities to escape responsibility for making such decisions themselves. Mandates also tend to shift attention from the more salient issues of purpose and pedagogy to those rooted in more familiar prose and politics. After all, bureaucracies and legislatures both prefer quantifiable solutions to more substantive and subjective ones.

Governmental Attitudes

Another adverse trend is the growing perception by state legislators and members of the U.S. Congress that universities are indistinguishable from other special interest groups seeking access to the public purse, with no intrinsically compelling claims beyond their political influence to affect the process and outcome. Such attitudes stand in stark contrast to an earlier time when American universities and colleges were perceived by lawmakers as special institutions in society with unique and indispensable capabilities, singularly able to educate the brightest of each generation, to advance the cause of knowledge and truth by invoking the scholarly norms of impartiality and objectivity, and by sharing what they know with society as a whole.

These legislative viewpoints are widely shared by the populace as a whole, and the public is not amused. There is public frustration, even resentment, with rising levels of tuitions and fees; with teaching loads, especially in leading universities, that are regarded as unreasonably low; with the perceived subordination of teaching to research; with college and university commitments to affirmative action policies and practices that are no longer supported by public opinion; and with the rise of political correctness within the universities themselves. These "realities" have come to be viewed by the public as betrayals of the social contract between the colleges and universities and the citizenry.

This social contract gave universities uncommon levels of autonomy in the administration of their internal affairs (e.g., admissions, curricula, degree requirements, tuition and fees, faculty appointments and promotions, and tenure) in return for an expectation that the costs to students would be attainable, applicants would be admitted or turned away based upon individual merit rather than group affiliation, teaching would be disinterested and have first call on the faculty's time and attention, and scholarship would be impartial. Only under these conditions, it was believed, could the university's role as a credible source of information, knowledge, and informed judgement be assured and the university's role as an authentic teacher of the young, rather than as a mere advocate for the jumble of personal biases of any given teacher or scholar, be secured. The fraying of this social contract has, in recent years, contributed to adverse public perceptions of American universities and has reduced the willingness of the voting public to fund them.

Structural Inefficiencies

Universities also possess structural inefficiencies that impair the prospects for adaptation and change. Examples of such inefficiencies include clinging to the familiar and to custom even though they are less well suited to the future than to the past; excessive preoccupation with prerogatives, especially in the academic departments; and, in a university's institutional relations, being driven by practice and turf rather than by synergies and new ways of cooperating and sharing to mutual advantage. One does not read of mergers or even joint ventures in higher education as one does in the corporate world.

Student Expectations

Another adverse trend is the incipient tension between student expectations and the colleges and universities in which they are enrolled. This tension is more dimly than clearly perceived by all parties, but it is there nevertheless. Today's students have a heightened sense of their own independence that is at odds with the institution's sense of its own authority. For example, the Western universities' sense of self is embodied within the history and customs of 800 years of university life. Such matters as the purpose of learning; the transmission of the culture from one generation to the next; the formulation and structuring of knowledge into a cohesive and credible curriculum; and the subordination of the student's judgement to the authority of the professor in such matters as required courses, pedagogy, standards, and evaluations are all regarded as within the authority and discretion of the university to define or decide, or, if disputed, to settle. But the students' view has become that of a consumer and, as with most consumers, the worth of what the university offers or requires is "priced" by students not so much within the academy's historic norms and values but more within the vocational or professional ambitions of the individual student.

The universities' awkward, but generally accommodating response, has been (1) to multiply vocational, pre-professional, and professional programs while shrinking the liberal arts and their place in the newer curricular schemes; and (2) to commercialize both its curriculum and much of its research, e.g., technology-transfer policies, patent and licensing policies, faculty leave policies, gift and grant policies, and linkages between universities and privately and publicly held corporations worldwide.

Learning Preferences

Finally, little systematic account is taken by faculty members, or university administrators and governing boards for that matter, of how today's undergraduate students prefer to learn. Thus, there is a disconnect between students who come to the universities steeped in technological, electronic, and other visually based methods of learning and a university pedagogy that is rooted more in the past than planted in the future, at least in the lower-division or pre-specialized programs and majors. Moreover, there has been an explicable, but barely defensible, institutional hesitancy in responding to distance learning possibilities and related issues bearing on the time, manner, and place of the teaching function, including the age and other changing characteristics of the student body.

CONCLUSIONS

These impediments to change, and others, will delay, but, in the end, will not prevent university reforms over time. But one should not fail to recognize that such changes, taken collectively, will have a profound effect on our colleges and universities, and not just on this or that aspect of university life but on the totality of its culture and its place in our society as well.

Bill Chace (1999), president of Emory University, in underscoring this prospect, recently observed that

> the change most important to the academy as a powerful medium by which values in our culture are expressed, modified and reinforced, is that the "hallowed" or "sacrosanct" idea of the campus is eroding. Where once professors and what they professed enjoyed both the prestige and the vulgar scorn of all those matters removed from the everyday nature of American life, they now are more and more a part of that life. They have been "desanctified.". . . Each such change can be understood, absorbed,

and explained. But the greater cultural landscape now looks different and will feel very different as the next decade approaches. . . . The groves of academe will bear the traffic of the world.

Account should also be taken of the universities in Europe, many of which are contending with the same issues, although within differing political, educational, economic, social, and cultural contexts. For example, European universities tend to find themselves over-enrolled, underfunded, over-regulated, and politicized. A pattern of faculty employed part-time, rectors and vice-chancellors exercising nominal authority for brief tenures, enrollment entitlements, tuition-free policies, state rather than university employment status, undue ministerial oversight, excessive bureaucracy, institutional separation of teaching and research, and almost exclusive dependence on state funding have all come to constrain, as well as to challenge, European universities seeking to change in a fast-moving world.

But the role European universities should play in the development of their respective countries, in the education of young people of talent, in the advancement and conservation of knowledge, and in the intellectual life of their respective countries is a widely shared and historic obligation, regardless of custom, law, and government.

The Western university has history on its side. Only a handful of institutions from the last millennium are with us as we move into the next one. The university is one of them. For it to remain as vital a force in the coming millennium as it has been in the last will require risk-taking, leadership, renewed confidence, and a greater willingness to reshape and realign its affairs and focus than is presently evident. Universities' historic role can only be placed in the broader service of humanity if they change with the rest of the world, thus remaining a credible, indispensable part of the ongoing life of our culture and a force for good and enhanced stability worldwide.

As the twentieth century closes, Americans need to be as bold, creative, and forward thinking about the university's future as were their predecessors during the last half of the nineteenth century. Americans should be reminded that others before them in the Western world, from the twelfth century on, somehow managed in the face of complacency, indifference, ignorance, and despair to raise the university's lamp high enough to illuminate not only the university's future but also its link to a more broadly civilized and cultured society.

REFERENCE

Chace, B. (1999). "Public Representation of Culture and History," forthcoming in a special issue of *The American Behavioral Scientist*.

CHAPTER 3

The Task of Institutions of Higher Education in the New Europe

Paolo Blasi

I n the next three years, 11 European countries will abandon their national currencies forever to adopt a common monetary unit, the euro. In the following years, the other four countries of the European Union will join the first 11 and become members of the "Euroclub."

Apart from the political and economic significance of the new monetary course, it is impossible to overrate the symbolic impact of the operation. Giving up their own national currencies—the historical symbol of national unity in recent times—citizens of individual states deprive themselves of a familiar instrument of daily life used by everybody in all kinds of transactions. Why have Europeans faced hardships and financial restrictions to achieve this goal? I believe that the establishing of an authentic European Union has been largely considered a priority, particularly in this age of change and instability, a situation that gives all political and economic problems a global dimension. In this perspective, the drive toward unity has prevailed. In my opinion, this happened because national monetary unity cannot any longer be identified as a cultural value essential to the identity of the citizens of a European nation. The loss of one's national currency is not felt as a *vulnus* to one's cultural identity if seen in the perspective of the defense and advancement of more significant common European values.

The situation of the various national systems—and particularly of institutions of higher learning, such as universities—is utterly different. Those institutions have evolved in different ways throughout the centuries and have made a substantial contribution to the diversity of the cultural traditions of the various states and regions of Europe.

The richness of this diversity must obviously be preserved—a view that is largely shared in Europe. The coexistence of different traditions and cultural values is the basis of that spirit of tolerance that is the life and soul of Europeans in their internal and external relations.

As to universities, three different systems can be, broadly speaking, identified in Europe: the Anglo-Saxon system, the French-Spanish system, and the German-Italian system. In the framework of each system, individual universities coexist with their own peculiarities. Yet some general views and values are common to all European universities.

A survey among the members of the Association of European Universities on *The European Universities in 2010* (1997) shows that the following main values are shared throughout Europe:

- Freedom of research and teaching must be the fundamental principle of university life.
- Research and teaching must remain inseparable at all levels of university education.
- The contribution of the university to the "sustainable development of society" will become the most important activity of such an institution.
- National governments should accept as much responsibility in higher education in the year 2010 as they do at present.

All this can be referred to the very origin of European universities. As a matter of fact, universities were created at the beginning of the second millennium inside Europe as transnational institutions with the purpose of developing a new comprehensive culture, adequate to the needs and problems of the new growing cities and consequently to the new economic activities and the new social interaction.

The university—bound *ad unum vertere*—combined the different aspects of human knowledge connecting culture and professional training in an all-embracing unitary Christian view of the human being. Later, the needs of the new philosophy of learning in the various specific fields of knowledge gradually brought about the differentiation of learning and the development of individual methodologies. Thus, Machiavelli maintained that the study of politics should be separated from the study of ethics. Later still, Galileo stated that the laws that rule the world of nature should be identified by an experimental method rather than by philosophical and theological arguments.

The division of learning into various branches and the application of the experimental method fostered, on the other side, the growth of science and technology to such an extent that humans, like so many new Promethei, are induced to the delusion of solving all problems through scientific progress. This delusion marked the positivist fad of the end of the last century and the first years after 1900.

Yet scientists themselves were the first to realize that science has its own limits. The theory of relativity in the first decades of this century represented a new approach to the conception of science. In the same way, artists will try to derive from the primitive world of Africa new inspirations that will find a common ground with the new stimuli created by the world of science.

Today, at the end of a century and a millennium, the European *Erlebnis* and the experience of the West in general are characterized by a widespread mistrust of science, and by a negative view shared by a significant sector of the young generation as to its applications. Such an attitude is obviously a consequence of the improper use of nuclear energy and bio-engineering—not to mention the dangerous impact on the natural environment of uncontrolled technological development. Humanity, and young people in particular, is now striving to recover stable values as points of reference. The need of a newly found cultural unity, rooted in the very nature of the human being, is deeply felt as a drive toward motivations of self-esteem and appreciation—a necessary condition for loving your neighbors as yourself.

The recent dramatic success of the film *Titanic*, particularly with the young generation, is, in my opinion, due to the authentic values that it represents. These values include the fragility of human technology in relation to the unpredictable forces of nature and, as a counterpart, the greatness of sentiments, of being in love, something of which humans are fully capable, something that can overcome not only the brutal violence of nature but also social and economic conditioning that can cause alienation in human beings. At the same time, young people today have to face a world subject to dramatic changes, a world where our know-how doubles every five years, where the very web of social structure is modified continuously, where stable jobs are on the wane, and where work conditions and professional abilities are renewed every day.

In past centuries, social change was slow and beyond the lifespan of any social being; an individual could perceive only a part of the process. Today evolving trends are daily modified in such a way that young people will necessarily face most of them during their lives. Young people must now become acquainted with the quicksand of an uncertain world, characterized by life conditions that are unlikely to last for long. Such being the case, their education and training, and, substantially, their cultural background, must be different from ours and adequate to the task. They will have to face new social problems, and above all they must be aware that individual behavior is relevant for everybody else. Globalization and the expanding progress of communication implies that each of us, with our behavior and our thoughts, can have an influence, direct or indirect, on other people everywhere in the world, almost in real time and without our even being totally aware of the process. All this calls for a deep renewal of education and training at the family, school, and social levels.

Above all, a European citizen involved in this new global context should be educated to a new concept of freedom. This freedom is not the liberty of doing anything one is willing to do, but freedom conceived as the ability of controlling one's behavior in view of the social significance it may eventually have. Last March, Dr. Benjamin Spock died. He was the guru of the laissez-faire educational philosophy as the right way of encouraging the expression of one's creativity. If this, in principle, were somehow justified as an attempt to break the reality of an excessive formal rigidity, there is no doubt that the consequences would be disastrous, as they have been wherever his principles have been adopted in American and European society.

The principle that the consent of the new generation is to be obtained at any possible cost, added to the laissez-faire philosophy, has been mischievous. Educators, both teachers and parents, have lost any sense of responsibility, inducing among young people the delusion of grandeur and omnipotence, and the incapacity for self-control.

Once forced to face the challenge and the hardships of life, a few of them give in and seek for security in drug addiction, or look for an identity in unconventional attire and attitudes; but they remain incapable of self-esteem and appreciation and of interacting with others. Thus, they will never become members of a well-ordered society and, even less, be equipped with the stamina to face a context full of uncertainties and continuous change.

I am aware that my analysis is oversimplified, more like a brief than a report. Yet I do believe that these reflections should go in parallel with the social and economic counterpart, if we are to define the aims and to plan the organization of universities so as to be in the position of confronting successfully the challenge of the coming century.

Everybody agrees that the most precious resource in the "society of knowledge" is the human being as such, the "producer" of knowledge, and, in the majority of cases, the processor, user, and communicator of knowledge. Humans are also capable of interpreting and integrating knowledge to transform it into patterns of behavior, decisions, and initiatives. As Malcolm Webb (1999), general manager for Human Resources of PetroFina SA of Belgium, said in a speech given at the Palermo Conference of the Association of European Universities,

> In order to survive and grow in the knowledge society, we need the help of well-rounded individuals with strong interpersonal skills who are not looking for a regimented or a controlled environment but are capable of living with uncertainty, keen to try to find solutions to complex problems

and committed to lifelong learning....[Industries] of course need people who are strong professionals in their particular domains. However, a technical expert who is insensitive to others, who cannot work in a team, and who will not share his or her knowledge is more of a hindrance than a help in modern industry.

Webb (1999) also identified the following "auxiliary skills" beyond academic achievement that today's graduates must have to be successful in their chosen professions:

- strong oral and written communication skills
- a basic understanding of mathematics and science
- good information technologies skills
- critical thinking ability
- an appreciation of the need for continuous learning
- the ability to work in teams
- creativity and initiative
- self-discipline, flexibility, and the ability to undertake sustained hard work
- an enjoyment of healthy competition
- cultural sensitivity and international awareness
- a result-oriented outlook and the ability to take decisions

Universities should plan their educational activities in such a way as to supersede the conventional tuition schemes once used to built up curricula and give priority instead to the reinforcement and development of the above-mentioned "auxiliary skills." Educational and academic curricula at all levels must take into consideration the importance of developing in the students such abilities and skills. Consequently, the organization and the procedures of the learning process in primary and secondary schools must be modified so as to substantially improve the basic background of college education. Therefore, it will be necessary to aim at a global methodological and critical training that may preserve its validity in the course of time, and be characterized by a philosophy that makes it the foundation of stints of specific, many-sided professional training.

How to achieve these aims? There is no doubt that conventional teaching is inadequate and that curricular restraints must be eliminated, and that interaction between student and teacher must take a new and less academic dimension. It should be taken for granted that auxiliary skills must develop at the same time between students and teachers. This implies that the prospective university teacher must be capable not only of doing research but of interacting satisfactorily with his or her students. A more active personal interaction between students and teachers requires adequate structures and a substantial staff increase if we think it necessary (as I do) to involve in higher education more and more young people. Today the European average is 40 percent of the age group.

All this means we must face the problem of financial resources and the priority of options by European governments and the European Union itself. These resources could be found by limiting agricultural investments as well as expenditures for the various national health systems. In fact, a new agricultural policy aimed at harmonizing the price of agricultural products to the standards of the world market, and at the same time prepared to give adequate recognition to the role of European agriculture for the safeguarding of the environment, could make reasonable resources available to finance a continuing system of higher education.

Those individuals who are endowed with a higher cultural level cost much less to national systems because they make better use of prevention and know-how to take advantage of what the public health facilities can offer. Further resources for education and training could thus be found. I am convinced that only a consistent and constant intervention by the governments could develop a university system of quality preserving the variety of the tuition modules and cultural identity, and at the same time offsetting the gap between the best universities and the less privileged ones. This is necessary if we want to encourage the balance of the cultural level and involve all social classes in higher education as it is happening in Europe right now. I also support the principle that students must share the cost of university education. In Italy today, they pay about 20 percent of the sums allocated by the government. This has a positive effect on students because it makes them aware of the cost of education and the value of activities and services offered by the university.

Another way of developing the students' auxiliary skills is experimentation with job activities inside the university, particularly if consistent with the careers they have chosen.

Universities must identify ways and means to foster this policy by involving an increasing number of students; by creating connections with the industrial, commercial, and agricultural world, as well as with society at large; by encouraging the employment of students for various jobs inside the university; and by ignoring the hostility of trade unions. Universities should become ever more open to all levels of society. In today's world, lifelong learning is a necessity. Universities are asked to play an extended and influential role in the education chain by greatly extending the work they undertake in the area of adult and continuing education; this extension is necessary for their own as well as for Europe's sake!

To satisfy the needs of continuing education, we must devise more flexible teaching structures and strategies. We can still have stable tuition facilities, like faculties and departments, but virtual and ad hoc structures should also be temporarily created to ensure that specific projects are realized. In the European system, characterized by a variety of options and decidedly diversified, only a large autonomy in organization, teaching, and finance can give an adequate answer to the above-mentioned problems. Thus, all European universities share the assumption that higher education should enjoy complete autonomy from the government and its rules, as well from the extramural world, including economic interests.

Yet the university cannot forget its own main task of being, above all, the natural cradle of spontaneous research, of cultural creativity, and of the transmission of learning that is not dependent on specific professional training. Students who ask the university to help them develop their intellectual callings still exist, and they should not be disappointed. They deserve particular attention because they may become our future colleagues.

The need to make a quality academic education available for a large number of students requires not only adequate resources but also high standards of research. Hence the choice of fields where a scientist may excel. Likewise, universities will find an identity in their specific task to amalgamate a global variety of knowledge and know-how.

Obviously, an academic institution excelling in all possible fields will never exist. Cooperation with other similar institutions must be encouraged so that networks may be created to share know-how and research projects in such a way as to put at the disposal of students learning facilities and qualified curricula. All this is possible and is happening already in Europe, where competition does exist, but without the extremes of U.S. academic life.

All this requires an internal organization of universities capable of giving an adequate answer to immediate problems while also being efficient and up to standards. Such an organization should guarantee academic freedom and should involve teachers and researchers in its various projects; it should also make proper use of its representative collegiate bodies.

We are facing a difficult but important challenge—how to reconcile the necessity of a sturdy individual leadership and the equally fundamental cooperation of collegiate bodies. The solutions being devised in Europe are various. It may be appropriate to take the initiative for an exchange of information that may favor "the best practice" and make it widely accepted, without interfering with the diversity of local situations and traditions and consequently with possible individual solutions.

REFERENCES

Association of European Universities/Utrecht University. (1997). *The European Universities in 2010*. Geneva/Utrecht: Association of European Universities, 66 p.

Webb, M. (1999). "Europe in a Period of Mutation and Change—The Role of Higher Education" in *A European Agenda for Change for Higher Education in the XXIst Century, Papers on Higher Education*. Bucharest/Geneva: UNESCO-CEPES/CRE action 111, pp. 25-34.

PART 2

. . . .

The Effect of the Changing Environment on Higher Education

CHAPTER 4

The Twenty-first Century University

A Tale of Two Futures

James J. Duderstadt

It was the best of times, it was the worst of times,
It was the age of wisdom, it was the age of foolishness,
It was the epoch of belief, it was the epoch of incredulity,
It was the season of Light, it was the season of Darkness,
It was the spring of hope, it was the winter of despair,

Charles Dickens, A Tale of Two Cities

To paraphrase Charles Dickens, these do indeed seem like both the best of times and the worst of times for higher education in the United States. On the one hand, in an age of knowledge in which educated people and their ideas have become the wealth of nations, the university has never been more important, and the value of a college education never higher. The educational opportunities offered by the university, the knowledge it creates, and the services it provides are key to almost every priority of contemporary society, from economic competitiveness to national security, from protecting the environment to enriching our culture. There is a growing recognition that few public investments have higher economic payoff than those made in higher education. In 1997, the federal government made the largest commitment to higher education since the GI Bill through $40 billion of tax incentives to college students and their parents as part of the budget-balancing agreement. In 1998, thanks to our unusually prosperous economy, Washington took further action by proposing the largest increase in the funding of academic research in decades. Both the administration and Congress promise balanced budgets and generous support for years to come.

Yet, despite this vote of confidence, there is great unease on our campuses. The media continues to view the academy with a frustrating mix of skepticism, ignorance, and occasional hostility that erodes public trust and confidence. The danger of external intervention in academic affairs in the name of accountability remains high. Throughout society, we see a backlash against earlier social commitments such as affirmative action, long a key mechanism for diversifying our campuses and for providing educational opportunity to those suffering discrimination in broader society. The faculty feels the stresses from all quarters. There is fear that research funding will decline again when the economy cools and entitlement programs grow. They are apprehensive about the future of such long-standing academic practices as tenure. They express a sense of loss of scholarly community with increasing specialization, together with a conflict between the demands of grantsmanship, a reward structure emphasizing research, and a love and sense of responsibility for teaching.

To continue paraphrasing Dickens, while we may be entering an age of wisdom—or at least knowledge—it is also an age of foolishness. Last year, the noted futurist Peter Drucker shook up the academy when, during an interview in *Forbes*, he speculated: "Thirty years from now the big university campuses will be relics. Universities won't survive. It's as large a change as when we first got the printed book" (Drucker 1997). One can imagine the reactions still ricocheting across university campuses following Drucker's conjecture. It was fascinating to track the conversations among the University of Michigan deans on electronic mail. Some responded by blasting Drucker, always a dangerous thing to do. Others believed it to be moot. A few surmised that perhaps a former president of the University of Michigan might agree with Drucker. (He doesn't, incidentally.)

So what kind of future do our universities face? A season of light or a season of darkness? A spring of hope or a winter of despair? More to the point, and again in a Dickensian spirit, is higher education facing yet another period of evolution? Or will the dramatic nature and compressed time scales characterizing the changes of our time trigger a process more akin to revolution?

To be sure, most colleges and universities are responding to the challenges and opportunities presented by a changing world. They are evolving to serve a new age. But most are evolving within the traditional paradigm, according to the time-honored processes of considered reflection and consensus that have long characterized the academy. Is such glacial change responsive enough to allow the university to control its own destiny? Or will a tidal wave of societal forces sweep over the academy, transforming the university in unforeseen and unacceptable ways while creating new institutional forms to challenge both our experience and our concept of the university? Returning again to Dickens, this could be a time when revolution is in the air!

In this chapter, we will discuss two sharply contrasting futures for higher education in the U.S. The first is a rather dark, market-driven future in which strong market forces trigger a major restructuring of the higher education enterprise. Although traditional colleges and universities play a role in this future, they are both threatened and reshaped by aggressive for-profit entities and commercial forces that drive the system toward the mediocrity that has characterized other mass-media markets such as television and journalism.

A contrasting and far brighter future is provided by a vision for higher education as a pervasive culture of learning, in which universal or ubiquitous educational opportunities are provided to meet the broad and growing learning needs of our society. Using a mix of old and new forms, learners are offered a rich array of high-quality, affordable learning opportunities throughout their lives. Our traditional institutional forms, including both the liberal arts college and the research university, continue to play key roles, albeit with some necessary evolution and adaptation.

Although market forces are far more powerful than my faculty colleagues are willing to accept, we remain convinced that it is possible to determine which of these or other paths will be taken by American higher education. Key in this effort is our ability as a society to view higher education as a public good that merits support through public tax dollars. In this way, we may be able to protect the public purpose of the higher education enterprise and sustain its quality, important traditions, and essential values.

If we are to do this, we must also recognize the profound nature of the rapidly changing world faced by higher education. The status quo is no longer an option. We must accept that change is inevitable and use it as a strategic opportunity to control our destiny, retaining the most important of our values and traditions.

FORCES DRIVING CHANGE

Powerful forces are driving an increasing societal demand for higher education products and services. In today's world, knowledge has become the coin of the realm, determining the wealth of nations. One's education, knowledge, and skills have become primary determinants of one's personal standard of living, the quality of one's life. We are at the dawn of an Age of Knowledge, in which intellectual capital—brainpower—is replacing financial and physical capital as the key to our strength, prosperity, and well-being.

As knowledge and educated people become key strategic priorities, our societies have become more dependent upon those social institutions that create these critical resources, our colleges and universities. Yet there is growing concern about the capacity of our existing institutions to serve these changing and growing social needs—indeed, even about their ability to survive in the face of the extraordinary changes occurring in our world.

The forces of change of most direct concern to higher education can be grouped into the following three areas: (1 financial imperatives, (2 changing societal needs, and (3 technology drivers.

Financial Imperatives

Since the late 1970s, American higher education has been caught in a financial vise (Dionne and Kean 1997). On the one hand, the magnitude of the services demanded of our colleges and universities has greatly increased. Enrollments have grown steadily, while the growing educational needs of adult learners are compensating for the temporary dip in the number of high school graduates associated with the post-war baby boom/bust cycle. University research, graduate education, and professional service have all grown in response to societal demand. Yet the costs of providing education, research, and service have grown even faster because these university activities depend upon a highly skilled, professional workforce (faculty and staff), require expensive new facilities and equipment, and are driven by an ever-expanding knowledge base.

While the demand for educational services has grown and the operating costs to provide these services have risen, public support for higher education has flattened and then declined over the past two decades (Breneman et al. 1997). The growth in state support of public higher education peaked in the 1980s and now has fallen in many states in the face of limited tax resources and competition from other priorities, such as entitlement programs and prisons. While the federal government has sustained its support of research, growth has been modest in recent years, and it is likely to decline as discretionary domestic spending comes under increasing pressure from the impact of unconstrained entitlement programs on federal budget-balancing efforts. Federal financial-aid programs have shifted increasingly from grants to loans as the predominant form of aid, reflecting a fundamental philosophical shift to the view that education is a private benefit rather than a larger public interest. While the 1997 federal budget agreement provides over $40 billion in tax incentives to college students and their parents over the next several years, much of this federal support is likely to go into new consumption rather than to enhance access to or support of higher education.

Increasing costs and declining public support have forced most institutions to increase tuition and fees. This has provided short-term relief. It has also triggered a strong public concern about the costs and availability of a college education, and it has accelerated forces to constrain tuition levels at both public and private universities (Gumport and Pusser 1997). Colleges and universities are looking for ways to control costs and increase productivity, but most are finding that their current organization and governance make this difficult.

The higher education enterprise in the U.S. must change dramatically if it is to restore a balance between the costs and availability of educational services needed by our society and the resources available to support these services. The current paradigms for conducting, distributing, and financing higher education may be inadequate to adapt to the demands and realities of our times.

Societal Needs

The needs of our society for the services provided by our colleges and universities will continue to grow. Significant expansion is needed for the 30-percent growth in the number of traditional college-age students over the next decade. In addition, an increasing number of adult learners in the workplace will be seeking the college-level education and skills necessary for their careers.

We are beginning to see a shift in demand from the current style of "just-in-case" education, in which we expect students to complete degree programs at the undergraduate or professional level long before they actually need the knowledge, to "just-in-time" education through nondegree programs when a person needs it, to "just-for-you" education, in which educational programs are carefully tailored to meet the specific lifelong learning requirements of particular students. The university will face the challenge of responding to other transitions: from passive students to active learners, from faculty-centered to learner-centered institutions, from teaching to the design and management of learning experiences, and from students to lifelong members of a learning community.

The situation is even more challenging at the global level, with over half the world's population under the age of 20. In most of the world, higher education is mired in a crisis of access, cost, and flexibility. Sir John Daniel, chancellor of the Open University of the United Kingdom, observes that although the United States has the world's strongest university system, the American paradigm seems ill-suited to meeting global education needs (Daniel 1996). Our colleges and universities continue to be focused on high-cost, residential education and on the outmoded idea that quality in education is linked to exclusivity of access and extravagance of resources.

Technology Drivers

As knowledge-driven organizations, colleges and universities should be greatly affected by rapid advances in information technology—computers, telecommunications, networks. In the past several decades, computers have evolved into powerful information systems with high-speed connectivity to other systems throughout the world. Public and private networks permit voice, image, and data to be made instantaneously available around the world to wide audiences at low costs. The creation of virtual environments where human senses are exposed to artificially created sights, sounds, and feelings liberate us from restrictions set by the physical forces of the world in which we live. Close, empathic, multi-party relationships mediated by visual and aural digital communications systems encourage the formation of closely bonded, widely dispersed communities of people interested in sharing new experiences and intellectual pursuits. Rapidly evolving technologies are dramatically changing the way we collect, manipulate, transmit, and use information.

This technology has already had a dramatic impact on our colleges and universities. Our administrative processes are heavily dependent upon information technology—as the current concern with the approaching date reset of Year 2000 has made all too apparent. Research and scholarship rely heavily upon information technology, e.g., the use of computers to simulate physical phenomena, networks to link investigators in virtual laboratories or "collaboratories," and digital libraries to provide scholars with access to knowledge resources. Yet, there is an increasing sense that new technology will have its most profound impact on the educational activities of the university and how we deliver our services.

We generally think of the educational role of our institutions in terms of a classroom paradigm, that is, of a professor teaching a class of students, who in turn respond by reading assigned texts, writing papers, solving problems or performing experiments, and taking examinations. Yet, the classroom itself may soon be replaced by learning experiences enabled by emerging information technology. Indeed, such a paradigm shift may be forced upon the faculty by the students themselves.

Today's students are members of the "digital generation." They have spent their early lives surrounded by robust, visual, electronic media—*Sesame Street*, MTV, home computers, video games, cyberspace networks, MUDs, MOOs, and virtual reality. Unlike those of us who were raised in an era of passive broadcast media, such as radio and television, they expect, indeed demand, interaction. They approach learning as a "plug-and-play" experience, unaccustomed and unwilling to learn sequentially—to read the manual—and inclined to plunge in and learn through participation and experimentation. While this type of learning is far different from the sequential, pyramid approach of the traditional university curriculum, it may be far more effective for this generation, particularly when provided through a media-rich environment.

Faculty of the twenty-first century may be asked to adopt a new role as designers of learning experiences, processes, and environments. Today's students learn primarily on their own through solitary reading, writing, and problem solving. Tomorrow's faculty may need to develop collective learning experiences in which students work together and learn together, with the faculty member acting as a consultant or a coach. Faculty members will be less concerned with identifying and then transmitting intellectual content and more focused on inspiring, motivating, and managing an active learning environment for students. This will require a major change in graduate education, since few of today's faculty members have learned these skills.

One can easily identify similarly profound changes occurring in the other roles of the university. The process of creating new knowledge—research and scholarship—is evolving rapidly away from the solitary scholar to teams of scholars, spanning disciplines, institutions, and even national boundaries. There is increasing pressure to draw research topics directly from worldly experience rather than predominantly from the curiosity of scholars. Even the nature of knowledge creation is shifting somewhat away from the *analysis of what has been* to the *creation of what has never been*—stressing the experience of the artist rather than the analytical skills of the scientist.

Emerging information technology has removed the constraints of space and time. We can now use powerful computers and networks to deliver educational services to anyone, anyplace, anytime, no longer confined to the campus or the academic schedule. Technology is creating an open learning environment in which the student has evolved into an active learner and consumer of educational services, stimulating the growth of powerful market forces that could dramatically reshape the higher education enterprise.

SCENARIO 1: A MASSIVE RESTRUCTURING OF THE HIGHER EDUCATION INDUSTRY

Universities have long enjoyed a monopoly over advanced education because of geographical constraints and their control of certification through the awarding of degrees. In the current paradigm, our colleges and universities are faculty centered. The faculty is accustomed to dictating what it wishes to teach, how it will teach, and where and when the learning will occur. This faculty-centered paradigm is sustained by accrediting associations, professional societies, and state and federal governments.

This carefully regulated and controlled enterprise could be eroded by several factors. First, the growing demand for advanced education and training simply cannot be met by such a carefully rationed and controlled paradigm. Second, current cost structures for higher education are incapable of responding to the needs for high quality yet affordable education. Third, information technology is releasing higher education from the constraints of space and time (and possibly also reality). And fourth, all these forces are driving us toward an open learning environment, in which the student will evolve into an active learner and empowered consumer, unleashing strong market forces.

Tomorrow's student will have access to a vast array of learning opportunities, far beyond the faculty-centered institutions characterizing higher education today. Some will provide formal credentials, others simply will provide knowledge, still others will be available whenever the student—more precisely, the learner—needs the knowledge. The evolution toward such a learner-centered educational environment is both evident and irresistible.

As a result, higher education is likely to evolve from a loosely federated system of colleges and universities serving traditional students from local communities into, in effect, a global knowledge and learning industry. With the emergence of new competitive forces and the weakening influence of traditional constraints, higher education is evolving like other "deregulated" industries, e.g., health care or communications or energy. These other industries have been restructured as government regulation has weakened. In contrast, the global knowledge-learning industry will be unleashed by emerging information technology that frees education from the constraints of space, time, and its credentialling monopoly.

Many in the academy would undoubtedly view with derision or alarm the depiction of the higher education enterprise as an "industry" or "business" operating in a highly competitive, increasingly deregulated, global marketplace. This is nevertheless a significant perspective that will require a new paradigm for how we think about postsecondary education. As our society becomes ever more dependent upon new knowledge and educated people, this global knowledge business must be viewed as one of the most active growth industries of our times. It is clear that no one, no government, no corporation, will be in control of the higher education industry. It will respond to forces of the marketplace.

Will this restructuring of the higher education enterprise really happen? If you doubt it, just consider the health care industry. While Washington debated federal programs to control health care costs and procrastinated taking action, the marketplace took over with such new paradigms as managed care and for-profit health centers. In less than a decade, the health care industry was totally changed. Higher education is a $180 billion a year enterprise. It will almost certainly be "corporatized" as was health care. By whom? By state or federal government? Not likely. By traditional institutions such as colleges and universities working through statewide systems or national alliances? Also unlikely. Or by the marketplace itself, as it did in health care, spawning new players such as virtual universities and for-profit educational organizations? Perhaps.

Several months ago, a leading information services company visited with my institution to share with us their perspective on the emerging higher education marketplace. They believe the size of the higher education enterprise in the United States during the next decade could be as large as $300 billion per year with 30 million students, roughly half of whom will be of today's traditional students and half adult learners in the workplace. (Incidentally, they also put the size of the world market at $3 trillion.) Their operational model of the brave new world of market-driven higher education suggests that this emerging domestic market for educational services could be served by a radically restructured enterprise consisting of 50,000 faculty "content providers," 200,000 faculty "learning facilitators," and 1,000 faculty "celebrities," who would be the stars in commodity learning-ware products. The learner would be linked to these faculty resources by an array of for-profit service companies, handling the production and packaging of learning-ware, the distribution and delivery of these services to learners, and the assessment and certification of learning outcomes. Quite a contrast with the current enterprise!

Unbundling

The modern university has evolved into a monolithic institution controlling all aspects of learning. Universities provide courses at the undergraduate, graduate, and professional level; they support residential colleges, professional schools, lifelong learning, athletics, libraries, museums, and entertainment. They have assumed responsibility for all manner of activities beyond education—housing and feeding students, providing police and other security protection, counseling and financial services, even maintaining campus power plants!

Today comprehensive universities—at least as full-service organizations— are at considerable risk. One significant impact of a restructured higher education "industry" may be to break apart this monolith, much as other industries have been broken apart through deregulation. As universities are forced to evolve from faculty-centered to learner-centered, they may well find it necessary to unbundle their many functions, ranging from admissions and counseling to instruction and certification. We are already beginning to see the growth of differentiated competitors for many of these activities. Universities are under increasing pressure to spin off or sell off or close down parts of their traditional operations in the face of this new competition. Many of our other activities, e.g., financial management and facilities management, are activities that might be outsourced to specialists. Universities, like other institutions in our society, will have to come to terms with what their true strengths are and how those strengths support their strategies—and then be willing to outsource needed capabilities in areas where they do not have a unique competitive advantage.

The Emergence of a Commodity Market

Throughout most of its history, higher education has been a cottage industry. Individual courses are a handicraft, a made-to-order product. Faculty members design from scratch the courses they teach, whether they be for a dozen or several hundred students. They may use standard textbooks from time to time—although most do not—but their organization, their lectures, their assignments, and their exams are developed for the particular course at the particular time it is taught. Our ability to introduce new, more effective avenues for learning—not merely new media in which to convey information—will change all that.

The individual handicraft model for course development may give way to a much more complex method of creating instructional materials. Even the standard packaging of an undergraduate education into "courses," required in the past by the need to have all the students in the same place at the same time, may no longer be necessary with new forms of asynchronous learning. Of course, it will be a challenge to break the handicraft model while still protecting the traditional independence of the faculty to determine curricular content. In this long-standing culture, faculty members believe they own the intellectual content of their courses and are free to market these to others for personal gain, e.g., through textbooks or off-campus consulting services. Universities may have to restructure these paradigms and renegotiate ownership of the intellectual products represented by classroom courses if they are to constrain costs and respond to the needs of society.

As distributed virtual environments become more common, the classroom experience itself may become a true commodity product, provided to anyone, anywhere, at any time—for a price. If students could actually obtain the classroom experience provided by some of the most renowned teachers in the world, why would they want to take classes from the local professor—or the local teaching assistant? In such a commodity market, the role of the faculty member would change substantially. Rather than developing content and transmitting it in a classroom environment, a faculty member might instead manage a learning process in which students use an educational commodity, e.g., the Microsoft Virtual "Life on Earth" course starring Stephen J. Gould. This would require a shift from the skills of intellectual analysis and classroom presentation to those of motivation, consultation, and inspiration. Welcome back, Mr. Chips!

Mergers, Acquisitions, and Hostile Takeovers

Looking at the future of higher education as a deregulated industry has several other implications. The more than 3,600 four-year colleges and universities in the United States are characterized by a tremendous diversity in size, mission, constituencies, and funding sources. Not only are we likely to see the appearance of new educational entities in the years ahead, as in other deregulated industries, but some colleges and universities will disappear. Others could merge. Some might actually acquire other institutions. One might even imagine a Darwinian process emerging with some institutions devouring their competitors in "hostile takeovers." All such events have occurred in deregulated industries in the past, and all are possible in the future we envision for higher education.

The market forces unleashed by technology and driven by increasing demand for higher education are powerful. If they are allowed to dominate and reshape the higher education enterprise, we could well find ourselves losing some of our most important values and traditions of the university. While the commercial, convenience-store model of the University of Phoenix may be an effective way to meet the workplace skill needs of some adults, it certainly is not a model that would be suitable for many of the higher purposes of the university. As we assess these emerging market-driven learning structures, we must bear in mind the importance of preserving the ability of the university to serve broader public purposes.

The waves of market pressures on our colleges and universities are building, driven by the realities of our times—the growing correlation between education and quality of life, the strategic role of knowledge in determining the prosperity and security of nations, the inability of traditional higher education institutions to monopolize an open-learning marketplace characterized by active student-learner-consumers and rapidly evolving technology. Driven by an entrepreneurial culture, both within our institutions and across American society, the early phases of a restructuring of the higher education enterprise are beginning to occur.

We need a broader recognition of the growing learning needs of our society, an exploration of more radical learning paradigms, and an overarching national strategy that acknowledges the public purpose of higher education and the important values of the academy. Without these, higher education may be driven down roads that would indeed lead to a winter of despair. Many of the pressures on our public universities are similar to those that have contributed so heavily to the current plight of K-12 education in the U.S. Furthermore, our experience with market-driven, media-based enterprises has not been reassuring. The broadcasting and publishing industries suggest that commercial concerns can lead to mediocrity, an intellectual wasteland in which the least common denominator of quality dominates.

SCENARIO 2: A CULTURE OF LEARNING

But there is also a spring of hope in our future. It is based on our inevitable and accelerating dependence upon knowledge and learning. We are beginning to realize that, just as our society historically accepted the responsibility for providing such needed services as military security, health care, and transportation infrastructure, education today has become a driving social need and societal responsibility. It has become the responsibility of democratic societies to provide their citizens with the education and training they need throughout their lives, whenever, wherever, and however they desire it, at high quality and at an affordable cost.

Of course, in one sense, this is just a continuation of one of the great themes of American higher education. Each evolutionary step of higher education has aimed at educating a broader segment of society, at creating new educational forms to do that—private colleges, the public universities, the land-grant universities, the normal and technical colleges, the community colleges. But today, we must do even more.

The dominant form of current higher education in the U.S., the research university, was shaped by a social contract during the last 50 years in which national security was regarded as the country's most compelling priority, as reflected in massive investments in campus-based research and technology. Today, in the wake of the Cold War and at the dawn of the age of knowledge, one could well make the argument that education itself will replace national defense as the priority for the twenty-first century. This could be the new social contract that will determine the character of our educational institutions, just as the government-university research partnership did in the latter half of the twentieth century. A social contract based on developing and maintaining the abilities and talents of our people to their fullest extent could well transform our schools, colleges, and universities into new forms that would rival the research university in importance.

So what might we expect over the longer term for the future of the university? It would be impractical and foolhardy to suggest one particular model for the university of the twenty-first century. The great and ever-increasing diversity characterizing American higher education makes it clear that there will be many forms, many types of institutions serving our society. But there are a number of themes that will almost certainly factor into at least some part of the higher education enterprise.

- *Learner-centered:* Just as other social institutions, our universities must become more focused on those we serve. We must transform ourselves from faculty-centered to learner-centered institutions.
- *Affordable:* Society will demand that we become far more affordable, providing educational opportunities within the reach of all citizens.

Whether this occurs through greater public subsidy or dramatic restructuring of our institutions, it seems increasingly clear that our society—not to mention the world—will no longer tolerate the high-cost, low-productivity model that characterizes much of American higher education today.

- *Lifelong Learning:* In an age of knowledge, the need for advanced education and skills will require both a willingness to continue to learn throughout life and a commitment on the part of our institutions to provide opportunities for lifelong learning. The concept of student and alumnus will merge. Our highly partitioned system of education will blend increasingly into a seamless web in which primary and secondary education; undergraduate, graduate, and professional education; apprenticeships and internships; on-the-job training and continuing education; and lifelong enrichment become a continuum.
- *Interactive and Collaborative:* We already see such new forms of pedagogy as asynchronous (anytime, anyplace) learning using information technology to break the constraints of time and space to make learning opportunities more compatible with lifestyles and career needs and interactive and collaborative learning appropriate for the digital age and the plug-and-play generation.
- *Diverse:* Finally, the great diversity characterizing American higher education will continue, as it must to serve an increasingly diverse population with diverse needs and goals.

We will need a new paradigm for delivering education to even broader segments of our society, perhaps beyond our society and to learners around the planet, in convenient, high-quality forms, at a cost all can afford. Most people, in most areas, can learn well using asynchronous learning—"anytime, anyplace, anyone" education. Lifetime education is rapidly becoming a reality, making learning available for anyone who wants to learn, at the time and place of their choice. With advances in modern information technology, the barriers in the educational system are no longer cost or technological capacity but rather perception and habit.

But this may not be aiming high enough. Perhaps we should instead consider a future of "ubiquitous learning"—learning for everyone, every place, all the time. Indeed, in a world driven by an ever-expanding knowledge base, continuous learning, like continuous improvement, has become a necessity of life.

Rather than "an age of knowledge," we could instead aspire to a "culture of learning," in which people are continually surrounded by, immersed in, and absorbed in learning experiences. Information technology has now provided us with a means to create learning environments throughout life. These environments not only transcend the constraints of space and time, but they, like us, are capable of learning and evolving to serve our changing educational needs. Higher education must define its relationship with these emerging possibilities to create a compelling vision for its future as it enters the next millennium.

EVOLUTION OR REVOLUTION?

Despite all evidence to the contrary, many within the academy still believe that change will occur only at the margins of higher education. They see the waves of change lapping on the beach as just the tide coming in, as it has so often before. They stress the role of the university in stabilizing society during periods of change rather than leading those changes. This too shall pass, they suggest, if we demand that the university hold fast to its traditional roles and character. And they will do everything within their power to prevent change from occurring.

Yet, history suggests that the university must change and adapt, in part to preserve these traditional roles. Many others, both within and outside the academy, believe that significant change will occur throughout the higher education enterprise, in each and every one of our institutions. Yet even these people see change as an evolutionary, incremental, long-term process, compatible with the values, cultures, and structure of the contemporary university.

A few voices, however, primarily outside the academy, believe that both the dramatic nature and compressed time scale characterizing the changes of our times will drive not evolution but revolution. They have serious doubts about whether the challenges of our times will allow such gradual change and adaptation. They point out that there are really no precedents to follow. Some suggest that long before reform of the educational system comes to any conclusion, the system itself will collapse (Perelman 1997).

As one of my colleagues put it, while there is certainly a good deal of exaggeration and hype about the changes in higher education for the short term—meaning five years or less—it is difficult to stress too strongly the profound nature of the changes likely to occur in most of our institutions and in our enterprise over the longer term—a decade and beyond. The forces driving change are simply too powerful.

Some colleges and universities may be able to maintain their current form and market niche. Others will change beyond recognition. Still others will disappear entirely. New types of institutions—perhaps even entirely new social learning structures—will evolve to meet educational needs. In contrast to the last several decades, when colleges and universities have endeavored to become more similar, the years ahead will demand greater differentiation. Many different paths will lead to the future.

For the past decade, we have led an effort at the University of Michigan to transform ourselves, to re-invent the institution so that it better serves a rapidly changing world. We created a campus culture in which both excellence and innovation were our highest priorities. We restructured our finances so that we became, in effect, a privately supported public university. We dramatically increased the diversity of our campus community. We launched major efforts to build a modern environment for teaching and research using the powerful tools of information technology. Yet with each transformation step we took, with every project we launched, we became increasingly uneasy.

We realized that the forces driving change in our society were stronger, more profound, than we had first thought. Change was occurring far more rapidly that we had anticipated. The future was becoming less certain as the range of possibilities expanded to include more radical options. We concluded that in a world of such dynamic change, as we faced a future of such uncertainty, the most realistic near-term approach was to explore possible futures of the university through experimentation and discovery. Rather than continue to contemplate possibilities for the future through abstract study and debate, it seemed a more productive course to build several prototypes of future learning institutions as working experiments. In this way, we could actively explore possible paths to the future.

Through a major strategic effort known as the Michigan Mandate, we significantly enhanced the racial diversity of our students and faculty, providing a laboratory for exploring the themes of the "diverse university." We established campuses in Europe, Asia, and Latin America, linking them with robust information technology, to understand better the implications of becoming a "world university." We launched major initiatives, such as the Media Union (a sophisticated multimedia environment), a virtual university (the Michigan Virtual University), and we played a key role in the management of the Internet to explore the "cyberspace university" theme. We launched new cross-disciplinary programs and built new community spaces that would draw students and faculty together as a model of the "divisionless university." We placed a high priority on the visual and performing arts, integrating them with such disciplines as engineering and architecture to better understand the challenges of the "creative university." And we launched an array of other initiatives, programs, and ventures, all designed to explore the future.

All these efforts were driven by the grass-roots interests, abilities, and enthusiasm of faculty and students. Our approach as leaders of the institution was to encourage a "let every flower bloom" philosophy, to respond to faculty and student proposals with "Wow! That sounds great! Let's see if we can work together to make it happen! And don't worry about the risk. If you don't fail from time to time, it is because you aren't aiming high enough!!!"

To be sure, some of these experiments were costly. Some were poorly understood and harshly criticized by those defending the status quo. All ran a high risk of failure, and some crashed in flames—albeit spectacularly. While such an exploratory approach was disconcerting to some and frustrating to others, many on our campus and beyond viewed this phase as an exciting adventure. And all these initiatives were important in understanding better the possible futures facing our university. All have had influence on the evolution of our university.

THE QUESTIONS BEFORE US

Many questions remain unanswered. Who will be the learners served by these institutions? Who will teach them? Who will administer and govern these institutions? Who will pay for them? What will be the character of our universities? How will they function? When will they appear?

Perhaps the most profound question of all concerns the survival of the university in the face of the changes brought on by the emergence of new competitors. That is the question raised by Drucker and other futurists. Could an institution such as the university, which has existed for a millennium, disappear in the face of such changes?

Most of us, of course, believe strongly that the university as a social institution is simply too valuable to disappear. On the other hand, there may well be forms of the university that we would have great difficulty recognizing from our present perspective.

Let me suggest a somewhat different set of questions in an effort to frame the key policy issues facing higher education.

1. How do we respond to the diverse educational needs of a knowledge-driven society? While the educational needs of the young will continue to be a priority, we also will be challenged to address the sophisticated learning needs of adults in the workplace while providing broader life-long learning opportunities for all of society.

2. Is higher education a public or a private good? The benefits of the university clearly flow to society as a whole. But it is also the case that two generations of American public policy have stressed instead the benefits of education to the individual student as a consumer.

3. How do we balance the roles of market forces and public purpose in determining the future of higher education? Can we control market forces through public policy and public investment so that the most valuable traditions and values of the university are preserved? Or will the competitive and commercial pressures of the marketplace sweep

over our institutions, leaving behind a higher education enterprise characterized by mediocrity?

4. What role should the research university play within the broader context of the changes likely to occur in the higher education enterprise? Should it be a leader in change? Or should it simply strive to protect the important traditions and values of the academy during this time of change?

AN ACTION AGENDA

So, where to next? How do we grapple with the many issues and concerns swirling about higher education? Let me suggest the following agenda for consideration and debate:

1. *Determine those key roles and values* that must be protected and preserved during this period of transformation, e.g., such roles as education of the young, the transmission of culture, basic research and scholarship, critic of society, etc.; and such values as academic freedom, a rational spirit of inquiry, a community of scholars, a commitment to excellence, shared governance, tenure, etc.

2. *Listen carefully to society* to learn and understand its changing needs, expectations, and perceptions of higher education, along with the forces driving change.

3. *Prepare the academy for change and competition* by removing unnecessary constraints, linking accountability with privilege, reestablishing tenure as the protection of academic freedom rather than lifetime employment security, etc. Begin the task of transforming the academy by radically restructuring graduate education as the source of the next generation of the faculty.

4. *Restructure university governance*—particularly governing boards and shared governance models—so that it responds to the changing needs of society rather than defending and perpetuating an obsolete past. Develop a tolerance for strong leadership. Shift from lay boards to corporate board models where members are selected based on their expertise and commitment and held accountable for their performance and the welfare of their institutions.

5. *Develop a new paradigm for financing higher education* by first determining the appropriate mix of public support (higher education as a public good) and private support (higher education as a personal benefit). Consider such key policy issues as (1) the appropriate burdens borne by each generation in the support of higher education as determined, for example, by the mix of grants versus loans in federal financial aid programs;

(2) the degree to which public investment should be used to help shape powerful emerging market forces to protect the public purpose of higher education; and (3) new methods for internal resource allocation and management that enhance productivity.

6. *Encourage experimentation* with new models of learning, research, and service by harvesting the best ideas from within the academy (or elsewhere), implementing them on a sufficient scale to assess their impact, and disseminating their results. Reward success while tolerating failure.

7. *Place a far greater emphasis on building alliances* among institutions that will allow individual institutions to focus on core competencies while relying on alliances to address the broader and diverse needs of society. Alliances should be encouraged not only among institutions of higher education (partnering research universities with liberal arts colleges and community colleges) but also between higher education and the private sector. Differentiation among institutions should be encouraged, while relying upon market forces rather than regulations to discourage duplication.

CONCLUDING REMARKS

We have entered a period of significant change in higher education as our universities attempt to respond to the challenges, opportunities, and responsibilities before them. This time of great change, of shifting paradigms, provides the context in which we must consider the changing nature of the university.

Much of this change will be driven by market forces—by a limited resource base, changing societal needs, new technologies, and new competitors. But we also must remember that higher education has a public purpose and a public obligation (Pew Higher Education Roundtable 1996). Those of us in higher education must always keep before us two questions: Whom do we serve? and How can we serve better? And society must work to shape and form the markets that will in turn reshape our institutions with appropriate civic purpose.

From this perspective, it is important to understand that the most critical challenge facing most institutions will be to develop the capacity for change. We must remove the constraints that prevent us from responding to the needs of rapidly changing societies, clear away unnecessary processes and administrative structures, and question existing premises and arrangements. Universities should strive to challenge, excite, and embolden all members of their academic communities to embark on what should be a great adventure for higher education.

While many academics are reluctant to accept the necessity or the validity of formal planning activities, woe be it to the institutions that turn aside from strategic efforts to determine their futures. The successful adaptation of universities to the revolutionary challenges they face will depend a great deal on an institution's collective ability to learn and to continuously improve its core activities. It is critical that higher education give thoughtful attention to the design of institutional processes for planning, management, and governance. Only a concerted effort to understand the important traditions of the past, the challenges of the present, and the possibilities for the future can enable institutions to thrive during a time of such change.

Those institutions that can step up to this process of change will thrive. Those that bury their heads in the sand, that rigidly defend the status quo, or, even worse, some idyllic vision of a past that never existed, are at great risk. Those institutions that are micromanaged, either from within by faculty politics or governing boards or from without by government or public opinion, stand little chance of flourishing during a time of great change.

Certainly the need for higher education will be of increasing importance in our knowledge-driven future. Certainly, too, it has become increasingly clear that our current paradigms for the university, its teaching and research, its service to society, its financing, all must change rapidly and perhaps radically. Hence the real question is not whether higher education will be transformed, but rather *how* . . . and *by whom*. If the university is capable of transforming itself to respond to the needs of a culture of learning, then what is currently perceived as the challenge of change may, in fact, become the opportunity for a renaissance in higher education in the years ahead.

REFERENCES

Breneman, D. W., Finney, J. E., and Roherty, B. M. (1997). *Shaping the Future: Higher Education Finance in the 1990s*. San Jose: California Higher Education Policy Center.

Daniel, J. S. (1996). *Mega-Universitites and Knowledge Media*. London: Kogan Page.

Dionne, J. L. and Kean, T. (1997). *Report of the Commission on National Investment in Higher Education: The Fiscal Crisis in Higher Education*. New York: Council for Aid to Education.

Drucker, P. F. (1997). Interview: "Seeing Things as They Really Are," *Forbes, 159*, pp. 122-28.

Gumport, P. J. and Pusser, B. (1997). "Academic Restructuring: Contemporary Adaptation in Higher Education" in Peterson, M., Dill, D., and Mets, L., eds. *Planning and Management for a Changing Environment: A Handbook on Redesigning Post-secondary Institutions*. San Francisco: Jossey-Bass, pp. 453-78.

Perelman, L. (1997). Interview: "Barnstorming with Lewis Perelman," *Educom Review, 32* (2), pp. 18-26.

Pew Higher Education Roundtable and California Higher Education Policy Center Roundtable on the Public and Private Finance of Higher Education (1996). "Shaping the Future," *Crosstalk, 4 (3)*, pp. 1-8.

CHAPTER 5

The University and the Information Age

Stanley O. Ikenberry

A mong the social and economic institutions to emerge over the past 900 years, few have survived as durably as colleges and universities. At least one explanation may be the ability of higher education institutions to adapt and change over the centuries. Certainly one need only look at the record of the last 100 years to document the magnitude of higher education's response to a rapidly changing society. Not just in the United States, but around the world, colleges and universities have adapted and changed while taking on new importance in the expanding information age. Globally, enrollments skyrocketed from 14 million in 1960 to some 82 million by 1995.

While it is almost certain that higher education institutions will continue to evolve in response to a rapidly changing and sometimes confusing world, the nature of the evolution, its speed, and its implications are far from clear. How higher education responds to the new information age and the complex communications capacity it brings with it may well shape the university in the next century.

Within this stark context, we hear such catchwords as "revolution," "paradigm shift," and "crisis," all of which may be accurate descriptions of the time in which we live. Knowledge is expanding; the capacity to generate, move, and respond to information is exploding; the workplace has become global; people are changing careers and roles more frequently; and, as a result, lifelong learning no longer is simply a desirable dream, it is an obvious imperative. For all these reasons, the premium placed on higher learning has grown dramatically.

Some have looked at this new world and predicted the demise of the university as we know it. Management guru Peter Drucker (1997) was recently quoted to that effect by *Forbes* magazine: "Thirty years from now, the big university campuses will be relics. Higher education is in deep crisis." Citing cost and access considerations, as well as the impact of new competitors and technological change, Drucker concluded that "universities won't survive."

Most of us have learned to take Peter Drucker seriously and to take notice when he speaks. Drucker may be right, but all my instincts, and the record of the last 900 years, tell me (to draw on Mark Twain) that the reports of our imminent demise are greatly exaggerated. Still, whether it is revolution or evolution, whether it is adaptation or demise, the forces are new—perhaps as significant as the invention of the printing press—and they are moving swiftly, with unprecedented consequences to be felt throughout the world.

One need only examine the worlds of commerce, entertainment, and global politics. Every day we witness the speed and power of communications technology and the expanded capacity to send, receive, and use information. More to the point, low-cost, high-power computing; communication networks; the Internet; Internet2; and countless other forms of electronic, digital, and telecommunications technologies literally are changing the way the world runs.

The *pace* of change is as remarkable as its consequence. In 1993, the Mosaic web browser was created at the University of Illinois and later incorporated into Netscape Navigator and Microsoft Internet Explorer. Now, millions of people have access to the web through these and other means. And all in only five years! But what about the next five years? We now have Abilene, the new Internet2 Protocol network, which will provide expanded capacity for such new applications as virtual laboratories, digital libraries, distance-independent education, and advanced networking.

Yet, focusing on the Internet alone obscures the reality and the vast impact of new computing and telecommunications technologies that range far beyond the net. In virtually every sector of our global society, the speed and power of communications technologies continue to grow. And the cost, at least in terms of speed and power per dollar, continues to drop.

The impact of this new technology has come more quickly and been more obvious in sectors other than higher education. Over the last decade, we have seen a virtual transformation in the world of finance. The continuing rush of bank mergers is made both possible and essential because of the new technology. The volatility of the world financial markets—driving currency values up and down and sending shock waves throughout equity markets—is attributable, at least in large part, to the power of communications technology. Businesses and corporations have reengineered their processes, in part because the new technology permits it, and in part because businesses require the new technology to remain globally competitive. And, we have seen transformations in the worlds of politics, entertainment, and journalism as well.

Change in higher education is coming more slowly, but it is coming all the same. And the consequences may be no less significant. One might even suppose that because colleges and universities are, in a sense, the ultimate "information age" institutions, the eventual impact of the new communications technology will be even greater in the academic sector than it is in others.

What is at issue? What is it about this new technologically driven information/communication age that is fundamentally different for the university? Some would answer, "very little." The life of the mind remains unchanged. The challenge, they would stress, is to comprehend, to analyze, to create, and to understand. The mission is to push back the frontiers of knowledge. All of that, it would seem, will remain the same.

The change, however, lies in the way information is moved, manipulated, and managed, and the ease with which access has been expanded. Already it is clear that new technology has caused colleges and universities to change the way teaching, research, and public service are carried out. Institutions are at different stages and are following different strategies with regard to technological infusion. In most instances, however, the revolution proceeds without any clear vision or master plan and many times is led by faculty and students who elect to change in response to new technological possibilities.

Whatever the plan (or lack thereof), on most campuses, access to the new computing/information technology is being made available, one way or another, to all members of the academic community. The way information is stored and shared is changing in classes and case studies, in accounting and enrollment systems, in university libraries and data banks. And along with all this has come a change in how colleges and universities allocate their resources, with increasing investment now devoted to acquiring technology, training individuals to use it, and hiring individuals to operate and maintain it.

COLLABORATION

While we see these technology-driven changes taking place, it is difficult to foresee their long-range implications. One already obvious consequence, for example, is a welcome increase in the capacity for collaboration. With the barriers of distance and time now less important, and with the cost of sharing information reduced, collaboration among scholars in different departments, with different work styles, and in different parts of the world has become easier. My son David, for example, on the faculty at Rice University in Texas, collaborates easily with his colleagues in Illinois, Paris, Hong Kong, and elsewhere.

Institutions are able to collaborate more easily as well. Administrative functions within and among institutions, for example, can be combined to increase efficiency and reduce costs. A single accounting department, purchasing department, or information center can serve multiple audiences and campuses in several locations. Library resources can be shared more conveniently.

So, for both individuals and institutions, as we worry about technology reducing our sense of community—our interrelatedness—there is also the possibility that technology will expand our sense of community and interdependence.

UNBUNDLING

A less obvious but ultimately more powerful consequence of the new technology is the opportunity it presents for "unbundling" learning objectives and desired outcomes. Over the centuries, the several functions served by higher education institutions have been accomplished together—teaching, research, and service are the most obvious of these.

Even within the teaching/learning mission, much of the "bundle" is not apparent. As part of a total learning experience, for example, residential campuses provide an environment in which young people grow and mature, a place where one can "find" oneself. Campuses offer a setting where values are taught and caught; where lifestyles are explored and formed; and where social, political, and economic beliefs are shaped, sometimes deliberately, but more often as part of a larger, quasi-random whole we call the campus community. At its best, a college or university enables students to "know," to "do," to "live and work" with others. Ultimately, higher education should enable its students to function effectively as complete human beings. This broader "bundled" view of learning—one that joins knowledge acquisition and skill development with personal growth and development—is what we think and speak of as the "purpose" of a college education.

To say that new communications technology permits the unbundling of these functions is, of course, true. But it does more than that. The new technology *invites* unbundling, partly because of economic incentives and realities, partly because of the needs and desires of those who are served, and partly because of the limits of the technology itself. As a result, teaching, or the sharing of knowledge and skills, tends to be unbundled from the creation of knowledge, or research. Likewise, information transmission tends to be separate from analysis and synthesis. As in health care, if it is possible to separate and recast the basic academic functions by using technology, what will this likely mean for colleges and universities a generation from now?

NEW PROVIDERS

The advent of new technology and the ability to minimize the barriers of time and distance, coupled with the surge in demand for learning in the new information age, have stimulated the emergence of new learning providers. To borrow a concept from the corporate world, the "barriers to entry" have diminished. One need not invest vast sums in bricks and mortar. One need not necessarily build an accomplished faculty or a vast library. Significant investments are still required, but they are of a different kind.

As a result, we are seeing a steady stream of new providers (and, therefore, new competitors) enter the higher education market. They include for-profit institutions, such as the University of Phoenix; new coalitions, such as the Western Governors University; and corporate universities, creatures of the business world.

The University of Phoenix is part of a publicly held, for-profit corporation, founded about two decades ago for the express purpose of serving working professionals, rather than the traditional, in-residence college student. Phoenix has unbundled the higher education market and has chosen to focus primarily on fully employed adults. Its current enrollment stands at more than 60,000, with numerous delivery sites around the country (and globally) along with online learning capacity. Accredited by the Middle States Regional Accrediting Association, the University of Phoenix admits only students who are 23 years of age or older and who are fully employed. In most cases, the student's employer pays for tuition, reflecting a closer link between learning and work.

The Western Governors University, or WGU, is a more recent creation, the brainchild of Utah Governor Mike Leavitt and Colorado Governor Roy Romer, who together worked to build consensus among the leaders of 16 Western states and Guam to create a new "cyber-university." WGU hopes to act in three capacities: as an electronic broker of distance-learning services on behalf of established colleges and universities within the region; as a vehicle for delivering training on behalf of corporations; and as a separate institution that itself will award degrees based on "competency assessment," rather than on the traditional, on-campus course credit and examination systems. In many ways, WGU is a broker, a new learning coalition driven by government.

Corporate universities have been around for many years, but the last decade has seen a dramatic surge of these new entities. Although no reliable statistics are available, it is possible that U.S. corporations now spend more money on education and serve more learners than traditional higher education institutions. Motorola, for example, reportedly spends some $120–$150 million annually. Arthur Anderson spends over 5 percent of its revenues on education and training. The typical corporation with a corporate university may spend 2 percent or more of its total revenue on this function.

The last decade has seen the number of corporate universities grow from some 400 to more than 1,000. For some corporations, the creation of a "university" is little more than a new name for an old function. For others, it is a recognition of the pace of change in knowledge. In still others, it reflects the requirements of global expansion and the need for common standards of performance and quality control.

Unlike traditional universities, these new creatures are not concerned with campuses, credits, degrees, or accreditation. And, like WGU and the University of Phoenix, the corporate university relies heavily on new technology as the education delivery vehicle of choice. The goal, whenever possible, is to deliver access to learning to the employee's desk or workstation.

Increasingly, students (and faculty) move back and forth between the corporate and academic worlds. The exchange between the two sectors is sufficiently significant that the American Council on Education offers a service called "ACE credit," which assesses corporate "courses" for potential transfer of credits to traditional colleges and universities.

QUESTIONS OF QUALITY

All of this, of course, immediately raises questions of "quality." In a world in which providers of information are ubiquitous, who (and what) is credible? When the information provider is a stable institution, with a faculty, a library, and a century-long reputation, the challenge of assessing quality is quite different from that of assessing the quality of a new-age, cyberspace learning provider. When learning is unbundled, how does one distinguish between the quality of data, information, knowledge, and wisdom, and the more important, long-range consequences of education about which we should care most? And, more interesting, to whom does it matter? Will we move to "accredit" learning products and systems rather than institutions and programs?

At this juncture, we have more questions than answers. For some, the new world of technology, including the advent of new competitors, offers excitement, answers long awaited, and opportunities to be exploited. Others greet the new era, if not with sadness, then with trepidation and a fear that the essence of what we know and value as higher education may be threatened. For most, the reaction is a cautious combination of both.

COMMERCIALIZATION OF LEARNING

New technology is obviously expanding access to information and learning. Within this environment, the economics of higher education are shifting.

Learning providers, for example, are likely to require a much larger scale of distribution for newly developed learning systems and products to make the initial investment in the new technology economically feasible. New corporations and new coalitions are almost certain to develop to create the capital necessary to exploit the new technology. And, correspondingly, new distribution coalitions and networks designed to capture the investment are likely to emerge.

Some see the prospect of an increasing "commercialization" of learning as a likely outcome of the new era. Existing higher education institutions, public and private, may not be structured in optimal ways for this new order. Individual faculty members working in isolated disciplinary departments in separate universities—the basic organizing units of the academic world as we now know it—are not the obvious building blocks in the new era. We may instead see teams of scholars, media specialists, system designers, and mass marketers, all with a capacity to take larger risks and move more quickly than has been possible within the traditional academic culture. Moreover, once "place" becomes less important in the new world of electronic communications and learning, the rationale for investment in higher education by state governments may change. In short, wholly new institutional forms and systems of financing may emerge, funded by private capital rather than by government.

QUESTIONS OF COST

One unfulfilled promise of the new technology has been that of cheaper if not better delivery of higher education. This potential advantage has not been lost on government; policymakers weigh the various priorities for public funds and look longingly at a new technology that might provide a quick fix to meeting the expanded demand for higher learning. In the first years of the twenty-first century, for example, the number of traditional college-age individuals is expected to rise, especially in the West, the Southwest, and the South. Some politicians and planners, including the Western Governors Association, look to the new technology to meet the demand for expanded access without the costs associated with a comparable expansion of the traditional delivery systems.

So far, however, the economic reality has fallen short of the dream. To date, application of technology in colleges and universities has tended to *add* to cost pressures, not relieve them. And yet, it is possible that over the long term substantial savings may be possible as we learn not just to add technology to an existing system of instruction, but to redesign the system itself, adding entirely new global delivery systems that reach vastly larger audiences. Only time will tell.

What all this means for institutions is less than clear. The impact and response may vary from campus to campus. Some small liberal arts colleges, for example, may be threatened by the new competitors, and others may find new life. If portions of the academic "content" were delivered via technology and available to the small liberal arts college, for example, and if faculty were to assume the roles of learning coaches, planners, and counselors, the new technology might give the liberal arts college a special competitive advantage. Such a campus could focus more on the development of the student as a person, and less on mere information transmission. For all institutions, the role of the library could take on a different meaning and be assessed in different ways if information resources were expanded to include global networks.

TRANSFORMATION?

What is the magnitude of change that confronts colleges and universities? The potential reach of the new technology seems almost without limits. Whatever the ultimate impact, technology has already changed higher education institutions—the way we organize ourselves, our policies, our culture, what faculty do, the way we work, and those we serve. And this transformation will continue well into the next century.

The big unknown is "place." Presently, while the academic world is changing, American higher education is still organized around the assumption that teaching and learning will occur in a defined place, through a direct personal exchange between scholar and student. The individual faculty member is the primary unit of investment, the principal means of delivery, and the main guarantor of academic quality. These fundamental assumptions are being challenged, and the traditional academic culture is likely to be the main object of transformation.

If higher education is to prove Drucker wrong, we must invent ways to capitalize on our strengths but alter our structure, our culture, and our methods of teaching and learning. We will be forced to define anew what we mean by "education." What learning do we hope to achieve? How will quality be assessed and judged? And, in the end, how will this new world be valued by the larger society? Institutions are almost certain to respond differently. Some will change dramatically, some only incrementally. The end result is likely to be a continuing increase in the diversity of higher education opportunities and options.

In time, we may learn that what appeared to loom so large at the end of the twentieth century will turn out to be but one more morsel that will be assimilated and digested by higher education with only modest lasting change. And yet, it may also be that we are in the early years of a sea change that will forever alter the history of colleges and universities and their relationship to society.

REFERENCE

Drucker, P.F. (1997). Interview: "Seeing Things as They Really Are," *Forbes*, 159, p. 127.

CHAPTER 6

The Economics of Higher Education in the United States

What Can Other Developed Countries Learn from It?

Harold M. Williams

Higher education is critical to the social and economic future of developed nations. This is more true now than ever before due to the exponential growth of technology, which requires a better educated workforce that is more flexible, more technologically sophisticated, and better prepared to address the complex problems of tomorrow's global economy and society. In addition, higher education opens the door to upward mobility to ameliorate the trend toward a locked-in, two-tier society. It allows members of disadvantaged groups to obtain the knowledge, skills, and credentials that will enable them to compete economically and achieve personal fulfillment.

However, at a time when higher education is in greatest demand, access to it is jeopardized as it becomes less and less affordable. A poll in 1990 reported that 88 percent of the American public believed that a high school diploma was no longer adequate to qualify for a well-paying job. Yet 87 percent believed that rising costs would put college out of the reach of most people.

Financial constraints are forcing both public and private institutions in the United States to radically change the way they operate. Total revenues simply no longer cover the cost of operating as they have in the past. We tend to think of the 1960s as the golden age in higher education, with the expectation that we will return to that period of prosperity. But it is now apparent that those days, not these, were the abnormal times. We must quickly find ways to meet the challenges of today's reality.

In response to diminishing public support, European universities, which are mostly publicly funded, are exploring ways to supplement with private-sector funds. In the United States, traditionally public universities rely more and more on private support. Based on the assumption that state support will continue to decline relative to demand and may eventually disappear, some publics are "privatizing," moving toward ultimate total dependence on private funds. As a result, these traditionally "publicly funded" institutions are now characterized instead as "publicly assisted."

Although the fees at public universities remain lower in absolute dollars, they mirror the tuitions of the privates and account for an increasing share of total revenues. And while private institutions still rely heavily on private support, private research universities depend heavily on federal research funding. For both publics and privates, nontraditional revenue sources, such as royalty income, are increasingly important.

It is apparent that financial equilibrium cannot be achieved without substantial change and restructuring. Tough questions must be answered: What can be forfeited? What can be shared? What can be changed? How can existing resources—such as the potential of the faculty, which is the core asset and the largest cost—be maximized?

An evolutionary response will not suffice. In the United States, research universities have adapted well over time, but not in step with a world that is changing at an unprecedented rate, particularly in technology and globalization. And stopgap measures have been exhausted. Inevitably, higher education must be restructured to survive.

In 1997, Peter Drucker predicted that because of uncontrolled expenditure, universities will not survive current socio-cultural and economic upheavals. Joel Elson (1992) concluded that without substantial improvement in the quality and content of higher education, the traditional college campus will disappear, replaced by distance learning and computer technology. Karen Arenson (1997) observed, "Welfare has had to change. Healthcare has had to change. The corporate world has had to change. Now it is higher education's turn."

THE DEMAND FOR HIGHER EDUCATION

Population growth is more of a factor in the increased demand for higher education in the United States than it appears to be in other developed countries. The U.S. is on the verge of a second-generation post-World War II population bulge. By 2002, the number of high school graduates will increase 14 percent; by 2006, 17 percent. California will experience an 18.3 percent rise by 2006, with a projected growth of 488,000 students.

Also unique to the U.S. is the rate of change in the racial and ethnic mix of American society and the need to ensure that the growing ethnic groups, particularly the Hispanic populations, have full access to higher education as they assume an increasingly significant role in American society and polity.

Perhaps more universal is the growing need for continuing education, particularly for studies that are not necessarily degree-oriented. As the demands of the workplace become more technological and more sophisticated, and as approaches to management as well as developments in the professions constantly change, lifelong learning becomes essential.

According to the U.S. Census Bureau, the number of adults aged 25 and older enrolled in college jumped 28 percent between 1987 and 1994 (United States Census Bureau, 1988-95). A recent study in California reported that a third of the students enrolled in the college systems already had a bachelor's degree and were returning to college for technical programs related to new employment opportunities. Perhaps as many as 20 million nontraditional students in the United States will be seeking additional higher education in the next decade. To what extent nontraditional institutions, rather than the colleges and universities, will ultimately meet this growing demand remains a question.

THE COST OF HIGHER EDUCATION

To the Student

Between 1975 and 1994, the cost of attending a private institution rose from 30 percent less than to 200 percent more than the median income for the American household. From 1975 to 1998, the cost of four years at a public institution rose from a third of median household income to the equivalent of median household income. Increased costs are forcing the middle class into public institutions and threatening to reinforce a two-tier society, with the less affluent—including much of the growing minority ethnic populace—pushed out.

The cost of a college education continues to grow in excess of increases in the cost of living. In 1998, private colleges and universities increased average tuition by 5 percent, and publics by 4 percent, while the Consumer Price Index (CPI) rose only 1.6 percent (United States Bureau of Labor Statistics, 1983–98). In the past 15 years, tuition costs have increased 195.3 percent while the overall CPI has risen just 63.3 percent. While recent increases in cost are less than those of the late 1980s and early 1990s, they are still too high. For most Americans, paying for college has become a daunting task. Loans now make up 60 percent of the financial aid available, with grants accounting for less than 40 percent. That ratio is almost exactly the reverse of 20 years ago. Institutions are drifting from grant-based to loan-based financial aid, causing many students to graduate with enormous debt obligations. As a result, many decide they can't afford higher education or are discouraged from considering less remunerative careers such as teaching or public service.

To the Institution

The public is generally unaware that, despite tuition and fee increases, the institution's cost of providing education, even in private institutions, significantly exceeds what it receives in tuition or public funding—a gap that grows annually and must be closed by funding from other sources.

While average tuition for private institutions rose from $10,040 in 1990 to $15,399 in 1997, an increase of 53 percent, net tuition, after discounts, increased only 33 percent. In fall 1997, 76 percent of entering freshmen received a discount averaging 49 percent of tuition. Further increases in tuition will produce proportionally less net revenue.

The "basket of goods and services" relevant to higher education (the Higher Education Price Index, or HEPI) differs from the components of the CPI. The fact that education is people-intensive accounts for perhaps half the difference. Most of the other half is caused by (1) high administrative costs necessitated by increased government demands and regulations and by the unwillingness of the federal government to fund the full share of overhead incurred in government-funded research activities and (2) expenditures necessary to compete for the best students, "faculty stars," and student amenities.

In addition, the number of faculty members has risen slightly faster than enrollments, and there has been an explosion in nonteaching staff. In fall 1976, universities across the U.S. had an average of 31.5 administrators for every 1,000 students. By 1993, the number had reached 51.4. By the mid-1990s, only about 35 percent of university employees actually taught students.

Instructional expenditures for each of the California public higher education segments increased dramatically from 1961 to 1990. At the University of California, expenditures per student increased 589.4 percent. Adjusted by the HEPI, the increase was 25.3 percent; adjusted by the CPI, the increase was 61.4 percent (United States Bureau of Labor Statistics, 1962–91). For the California State University, the increases, respectively, were 444 percent, 10.5 percent, and 32 percent. For the community colleges, the changes were 413.2 percent, minus 6.6 percent, and 20.1 percent.

Currently, 78 percent of college- and university-level students in the United States attend public universities. Excluding community colleges, 66 percent attend public institutions. Given the competing demands on public tax revenues for health, welfare, prisons, etc., the percentage share of state revenues being devoted to higher education is decreasing. For example, at the University of California, revenues from the state increased 16 percent in the decade from 1988 to 1998—far less than the CPI, let alone the HEPI. The U.C.'s share of state revenues dropped from 5.72 percent to 4.11 percent during the period, while its enrollment increased by 7 percent, and student fees tripled. Given present trends, the university's share of state revenues can be expected to decline further. Yet, if more were invested in higher education today, less expenditures would be required to treat social ills in the future. The balance between state revenues devoted to current societal needs and investments in the economic and social future of the state are disproportionately tilted toward the former.

THE RESPONSE OF HIGHER EDUCATION

Without limiting access by restricting admission or increasing tuition, higher education is forced to contain its costs. With public pressure to cap the growth of tuition, the focus has shifted to cost control. Administrative and service costs were addressed first. Random reduction in faculty and academic support followed. Some institutions have focused on areas of excellence and discontinued marginal programs. Some have hired lower-cost, younger, and part-time faculty and increased teaching loads and class sizes. But these measures will not contain the underlying pressures to increase costs and will not support structural changes that might alleviate the pressures. Overall, there seems to be a lack of institutional mechanisms to set priorities or make judgments about reductions.

Will "privatizing" work for public institutions? Becoming more like private higher education will not solve the problem, although it may provide some interim amelioration. Can other sources of revenue be generated to close the gap over time? I do not believe so. Can the HEPI be brought down so that the real cost does not increase more than consumer purchasing power? Not unless faculty members are engaged more efficiently.

Ultimately, the fiscal problems can be addressed only by basic changes within higher education. Reducing per capita expenditures significantly will require fundamental rethinking. The governance structure must be changed to enable the essential institutional-level investment and trade-off decisions to be made so that leaders can assess the relative value of departments, programs, and systems to reallocate scarce resources, streamline services, and respond to the changing needs of their constituencies. In the corporate world, a number of chief executives have been accused of short-term thinking and decision making on the premise that they will have retired before "the deluge." To what extent is this also true of leadership in higher education? Yet it must be noted that the ability of leadership is severely constrained by the decentralization of decision making, the process of shared governance, tenure, and the conflicting loyalty of faculty to discipline rather than institution.

The report of the Commission on the Academic Presidency (1996), on which I served, entitled *Renewing the Academic Presidency—Stronger Leadership for Tougher Times*, recommended that shared governance can and should be maintained—but not in its present imprecise, undisciplined form. It must be clarified and simplified so that those with the responsibility to act can exercise the authority to do so. Shared governance cannot ensure that all parties will agree on all issues.

Any proposal that can be interpreted as an effort to increase productivity is met with intense opposition. The conventional view is that higher education cannot achieve increases in productivity without a loss in quality any more than a chamber music trio could increase productivity by playing more rapidly or eliminating one of the players.

Nevertheless, the faculty must be enabled to be more productive. The solution lies in using the faculty in the most effective way as *one* of the resources available in the learning process. We have learned so much about the different ways in which students learn, and yet we continue to focus more on teaching than learning. Increasing teaching loads and class sizes and substituting lower-cost younger and part-time faculty for more expensive senior faculty are not the ultimate answer and will not produce the necessary gains in productivity. None of these approaches challenges the fundamental assumption that faculty members meeting with groups of students at regularly scheduled times and places is essential to achieve effective student learning. This assumption underlies the entire organizational framework for higher education, affecting everything from course accounting and faculty workload to tuition and state funding.

Information technology enables education to move away from synchronous learning. Faculty, while the most essential, are only one of many resources important to learning. Pedagogical opportunities need to be explored and applied. The focus has to shift from teaching to learning and from time to results. The role of technology lies not so much in the technologies themselves but in how they are employed to enhance learning. Information technology can reposition and revitalize teaching, much as it already impacts research. The real advantage of technology is its ability to transform pedagogy and extend the use of faculty while preserving, and perhaps increasing, quality of learning, student/faculty contact, and inter-university collaboration.

While distance education expands the ability of current programs to reach off-campus populations, this is not the greatest potential of information technology. Rather it is to challenge the assumption that education must take place in classrooms where professors teach groups of students. It is now feasible to distribute contents and allow high levels of interaction between and among teachers and students without requiring schedules to be synchronized. Non-synchronous education, already common in doctoral programs, can now be available to all students.

The cost structure for technology-mediated instruction is different than for traditional classroom-based courses. For the latter, the cost is mostly the salary of instructors and the expense of their support services. Especially in larger institutions, the marginal costs of traditional instruction are close to the average costs. And costs tend to remain constant over time except for incremental increases to keep up with inflation, and salary increases in excess of inflation. In contrast, costs for technology-mediated instruction are more akin to those of software development. Up-front costs for development are relatively high but the expense of ongoing delivery can be lower than for classroom instruction. Development costs can be amortized over the period in which a course or program is used, which could be several years. Periodic modification involves less cost.

Faculty must be expected and enabled to employ technology and pedagogy to enhance student learning. This needs to be an institutional policy and priority with leadership from the president. Examples of effective pedagogy can be found at most institutions but they remain marginalized to the dominant mode of lecture-based, didactic instruction. Incentives can encourage re-design of instructional approaches to achieve cost savings as well as quality enhancements through technology. The approach to budgeting for such change will need to be modified because it is difficult to fit the costs of technology-mediated programs into annual budget cycles.

Another area that must be re-examined is the system of faculty rewards and incentives. We must raise the status of teaching with commensurate award. We must rethink faculty appointments and the commitments that faculties and institutions make to each other. This rethinking could well lead to reconsideration of the criteria for tenure and for long-term, nontenure track appointments. It also requires that we produce Ph.D.s who are qualified and prepared to participate in such a changing higher education environment.

While technology can easily extend access to higher education to new populations at lower cost than traditional classroom instruction, the real question is whether higher education will organize itself to maximize the potential benefits of technology in quality, access, and cost. Unless and until that happens, technology just represents an additional expense. Once *learning* becomes the central focus, the response centers on how best to use *all* available resources to produce the most effective results for the most people. That must be the objective if society is to have the access to higher education that it expects and deserves.

REFERENCES

Arenson, Karen. (August 31, 1997). "Rationing Higher Education," *New York Times*, pp. iv (1).

Commission on the Academic Presidency. (1996). *Renewing the Academic Presidency—Stronger Leadership for Tougher Times*. Washington, D.C.: Association of Governing Boards of Universities and Colleges.

Drucker, P.F. (1997). "Interview: Seeing Things As They Really Are," *Forbes, 159*, pp. 122–28.

Elson, Joel. (April, 1992). "Education: Campus of the Future," *Time*, p. 54.

United States Bureau of Labor Statistics. (1962–91). *Consumer Price Index*. Washington, D.C.: U.S. Government Printing Office.

United States Bureau of Labor Statistics. (1983–98). *Consumer Price Index*. Washington, D.C.: U.S. Government Printing Office.

United States Census Bureau. (1988–95). *School Enrollment—Social and Economic Characteristics*. Washington, D.C.: U.S. Government Printing Office.

PART 3

• • • • • • • • • • • •

Meeting the Challenge

CHAPTER 7

Financing Universities Through Nontraditional Revenue Sources
Opportunities and Threats

Werner Z. Hirsch

I n 1966, Walter Lippmann wrote, ". . . there has fallen on the universities a unique, indispensable and capital function in the intellectual and spiritual life of modern society" (Hollinger 1996). Nonetheless, in the 1990s, governmental funding of universities, especially public research universities, declined significantly. To describe today's problems of higher education in many Western industrialized countries, dramatic words are often used: crisis, turmoil, disarray, collapse. These nouns are probably exaggerations, but many observers would agree that higher education throughout the industrialized Western world today faces great fiscal challenges. This is puzzling, particularly when, like Walter Lippmann, so many political leaders point to the great value of a well-educated population and the pivotal role of higher education in society's future.

The effects of the present fiscal difficulties, particularly of public research universities, should, in the words of Dr. Johnson, "concentrate the mind" of leaders in academia and energize them to rise to introduce innovations into the governance, planning, and operation of the university as well as its financing.

Many factors can be held responsible for the present financial troubles of most universities, both in Western Europe and North America. The decline in government support is one important factor, but not the only one. Research, and with it graduate education, has become increasingly costly, particularly in the sciences, where ever more expensive equipment has become a necessity. Also, government regulations and reporting requirements have become more onerous.

In spite of financial pressure, universities have done relatively little to become more efficient, at a time when many businesses have aggressively "reinvented" themselves and have thereby increased their productivity. They did so by outsourcing many services, effectively using information technology, downsizing their staff and labor force, and arranging for part-time employment. Except for part-time faculty, universities have done relatively little to reinvent themselves. Many have even gone in the opposite direction from outsourcing. Instead, they own today a host of business enterprises—hospitals, bus and van transportation systems, faculty housing, guest houses and hotels, commercial rentals, health centers, power plants, etc. Clearly most universities have little experience and competence in such undertakings, all of which are far removed from their missions of teaching and research. Cutting back on nonacademic undertakings or outsourcing them could serve universities well.

Financing higher education is the topic that both Harold Williams (Chapter 6) and I address, with my focus on the development by universities of nontraditional funding sources. The search for income from such sources has gained momentum, particularly in public research universities, to compensate for declining government support and rising operating costs.

It is useful to divide these new university funding sources into first and second generation, depending on when they were introduced. The major source of the first type is private giving, increasingly involving mega-dollar campaigns. Such solicitation is certainly not new, but it has skyrocketed in recent years in the United States; some universities are engaged in raising more than a billion dollars each in 5- to 7-year campaigns.

Second generation nontraditional income sources include corporate sponsorship of university research; commercialization of university-owned intellectual property resulting in royalties and licensing fees, as well as the establishment of joint start-up venture companies; university-owned business enterprises; and joint university-private sector commercial enterprises.

This chapter will start with a review and discussion of first and then second generation nontraditional income sources. The focus will be on income-raising activities, their productivity, costs, and potential for being at odds with the university's academic mission. Having identified the nature of the threat these nontraditional funding sources pose to the university, safeguards will be suggested and their respective merits examined. This evaluation will be guided by the university's need to balance the productivity of the different funding sources with their likelihood of compromising its academic mission.

At this time, a disclaimer is in order. It would be a mistake to assume that efforts that raise income from second generation nonconventional sources have money as their sole purpose. Another objective is for the research university to assist in technology transfer and commercialization of university-developed and owned intellectual property, and in building alliances with high-tech industries to contribute to regional and national economic growth and prosperity. Thus, the chapter will examine the munificent effects second generation university–industry alliances can have on high-income regional employment growth and national economic growth and prosperity; and that therefore, governments are well advised to fund research universities generously.

FIRST GENERATION FUNDING SOURCES

Mega-Dollar Gift Campaigns

Universities and colleges have long been the recipients of private giving, but in recent years the pace of fundraising efforts by university officials has sped up significantly. For example, two University of California campuses have been engaged in fundraising campaigns with more than $1 billion as targets. Harvard University has a $2.1 billion goal. Between 1990 and 1995, private funds raised by American universities and colleges increased by 30 percent to $12.7 billion in 1995. Alumni contributions increased 42 percent, accounting for more than those of any other group (Breneman and Finney 1997).

Large-scale fundraising activities by universities involve what economists call high transaction costs. Some are monetary in terms of large fundraising staffs. But perhaps the more significant costs involve the time spent by presidents and chancellors in fundraising rather than in guiding and inspiring academic endeavors. For example, the chancellor of one of the premier public research universities indicated to me that he spent 40 percent of his time raising private funds. And William Bennett, President Ronald Reagan's secretary of education, in pondering the Clinton sex scandal, is reported to have said, ". . . prosperous America enjoys life too much to care. . . .Where are the clerics and where are the university presidents? Hah! Raising money!" (Lexington 1998).

Moreover, private giving as an income source can unbalance the academic program. Universities find it much easier to raise funds for medicine or molecular biology, for example, than for classics and the fine arts. Understandably, they are reluctant to reject large gifts, even those that are likely to have unsettling academic effects.

Furthermore, for the sake of pleasing alumni and ensuring their beneficence, universities often engage in activities unrelated to their primary mission, and possibly even in conflict with it. The emphasis on intercollegiate athletics, especially football and basketball, falls into this category. Such teams are often barely distinguishable from for-profit professional teams, designed more to assure donors' loyalty than to build character. Sports programs can interfere with students attending classes and acquiring an education, and can result in salary distortions. For example, the 1997-98 pay package of the UCLA basketball coach was $445,000, whereas the chancellor's was $223,000 and the California governor's $131,000 (Shelton 1998).

SECOND GENERATION FUNDING SOURCES

Corporate Research Support, Patents, Licensing, Commercialization

Though gifts have grown, they have not kept up with rising budget needs of universities and colleges. In response, institutions are pursuing funding sources that require great entrepreneurship and move them into an altogether foreign area that has its own dynamics. Corporate university research support nearly quadrupled between 1980 and 1989, from $238 million to $920 million (Grassmuck 1990). When grants produce valuable research findings, decisions must be made about patent rights, about whether to license the results, and, if so, how license fees are to be divided, and whether to found a jointly owned (and possibly jointly operated) start-up venture. In 1997, American and Canadian universities awarded 2,741 licenses to private firms (University of California 1997).

A survey of 173 universities and colleges revealed that with a 1996 research budget of $21.4 billion, they collected $592 million from patents and licenses, up 167 percent in five years. The leader was the University of California, which earned $63.8 million from patents and licenses, followed by Stanford with $43.8 million and Columbia with $40.6 (Markus 1998).

Rather than licensing their patents to industry, universities often make participatory arrangements, e.g., start-up investments, in cooperation with private firms. This development may have been helped along by a report by SRI International for the National Science Foundation. Based on this report, Gregory and Sheahen (1991) concluded that start-up investments are more successful and lucrative than the licensing of university patents.

While a number of interesting efforts have been mounted, perhaps the leader in industry–university partnership is the CONNECT program of the University of California at San Diego. This program is credited with having nurtured, with university research and assistance, about 120 high-tech companies in the San Diego area. The result has been the employment of about 15,000 people and an annual revenue of nearly $2 billion (Atkinson 1998).

University-Owned Commercial Enterprises

In recent years, universities have increasingly undertaken many commercial activities on their own. They have acquired more and more auxiliary enterprises and housekeeping functions, and have built the infrastructure to support them. Such steps are taken at a time when business and some governments have been going in the opposite direction, i.e., sourcing out or contracting out such activities. The magnitude of universities' expenditures for these nonacademic activities is large. Research universities seem to spend only about half their overall budgets on instruction and research and the other half on a host of auxiliary enterprises and housekeeping functions. For example, four campuses of the University of California without teaching hospitals spent 45 to 49 percent of their 1996-97 budgets on activities other than instruction and research. At UCLA, which has a teaching hospital, that percentage was 60.

In relation to some commercial enterprises, universities are their own customers; in others, they have outside clients. For example, when land or office and residential properties are donated, the university can become a landlord and, though inadvertently, a player in the real estate market. After the promise of scale economies persuades it to invest in additional real estate, the university often learns belatedly the difficulties faced by landlords.

The scope of university-owned commercial enterprises has been expanding rapidly and sometimes into unusual areas. Harvard University, with an endowment of about $13 billion, has invested in the stock market, real estate, and oil and gas exploration. Most recently, it purchased the White River Corporation, an insurance services and investment firm, for $400 million (Putka 1997). These investments are clearly associated with significant risk.

Joint University—Private Sector Commercial Enterprises

Universities increasingly enter contracts with private firms designed to produce income. A venerable practice is the sale of the right to use a university's logo on T-shirts, caps, etc. More recently, the University of British Columbia has chosen, for a fee, to use a single airline and bank (Economist 1998). Such arrangements tend to be inefficient and also costly to customers because of lack of choice and possibly higher monopoly prices.

Advances in information technology are opening up further opportunities for joint ventures between universities and high-tech industries. One such venture was an ambitious proposal for a California Educational Technology Initiative (CETI) which had a $4 to $5 billion potential to the companies. However, after years of negotiations, the CETI was abandoned (Chapman 1998). Many questions have been raised regarding such arrangements, particularly since faculty members fear that their copyrights to course material may not be properly safeguarded. These fears are fanned by controversies surrounding many of the partnerships between universities and private corporations in distance learning networks.

CHALLENGES AND DANGERS

The pursuit of nontraditional funding sources and the chain of events that can ensue pose serious challenges to universities in an often entirely unaccustomed arena. Historically, faculty members have engaged in researching subjects of intellectual interest to them. Today, some faculty members worry that this search for new knowledge will be compromised by corporate sponsorship. Will research universities induce or even pressure their faculty to focus on areas likely to prove profitable? If so, will the metaphor of a corporation's and faculty's interest being approximated by circles that overlap in places, be replaced by one of a linear relationship? In the latter case, the corporation would tell faculty what specific research must be selected to be funded. Will these close ties between the research university and the corporate world then transform universities into private sector laboratories, heavily focused on potentially profitable research? Some believe they can already observe ominous signs. They point to universities agreeing to contract clauses that are increasingly congenial to corporate sponsors, including pre-invention license agreements, publication delays, pre-publication access to research results, and censorship. Others point to research laboratories built by private firms on university campuses to which faculty have no access.

Patents and licensing also can cause frictions within universities about patents and licensing fee distribution among inventor, department, and university. Dissatisfied inventors can leave universities to set up their own corporations, taking with them the best graduate students. But even satisfied faculty members tend to set up their own corporations, or consult for corporations while reducing their commitment and time given to the university. Universities must develop carefully crafted policies regarding conflict of interest and commitment, tenure, and consulting practices. The Harvard Medical School has done so. Moreover, ownership of intellectual property rights is often a bone of contention. Do they belong to the university or to the corporation? Court fights are not uncommon (Science 1998).

The challenges are even greater with regard to jointly owned (and operated) start-up ventures. Opportunities for conflicts of interest seem endless. For example, according to Matkin (1994),

> Several major research universities, including Harvard, Johns Hopkins, the University of Chicago, and Boston University, have found that investments in start-up companies are often costly to the university in terms of both economy and public relations. For example, the president and several members of the board of trustees of Boston University (BU) have been under investigation for conflict of interest involving the university's investments in start-up companies such as Seragen Incorporated, which was founded in 1987 to develop some intellectual

property owned by BU, and that received most of its funding from BU until it went public in 1992. John Silber, BU's president, is a director of the company and owns 105,000 shares. He also may have made $386,700 when a Seragen spin-off company, Seradyn, was sold. Several members of the board of trustees were involved in Seragen.

The cold fusion controversy at the University of Utah, clearly caused by the university's desire to realize a large financial return, resulted in a great deal of. . . damage to its academic reputation, and may have led to the resignation of the university's president when it was discovered that he had improperly transferred funds to support cold fusion development. Michigan Technological University's Venture Group, Incorporated, a profit-seeking investment company, has been controversial since it lost $1.6 million in 1989 because of mismanagement and embezzlement by its officers. The University of South Carolina's research and development foundation has been under intense public scrutiny since 1987, and this scrutiny led to indictments and convictions against the university's former president, James B. Holderman.

INITIATIVES TO ABATE DANGERS

The preceding discussion has pointed to the hazards academic institutions face when they become part of and enmeshed in the world of commerce. Entering such a world can cause culture shock and serious tension among the administration, faculty, governing board, and such other interests as alumni and students.

To keep these risks in bounds, universities, particularly public research universities, face three serious challenges. They must

- avoid arrangements that can compromise fulfillment of the university's mission and thereby debase the academic enterprise
- avoid conflicts of commitment and interest
- avoid the appearance of unfair advantage

Undertakings at odds with the university's mission and those that can lead to conflicts of interest and commitment have already been discussed. A few comments about unfair advantage, whether real or imaginary, are in order. They mainly relate to public institutions because much of their research funding comes from government sources. Unfairness is often alleged to exist when such institutions engage in fundraising on a large scale in competition with private universities and colleges. The charge of unfairness is also levelled in connection with patents, license fees, and other income-earning arrangements gained from research by faculty. Public research universities, in the eyes of many citizens and legislators, are not entitled to gain income from knowledge produced by faculty whose salary is paid to a large extent from taxes collected by government. Yet, government support of public research universities in the United States has steadily declined. For example, state funding has declined from 27 percent of their budget in 1990-1991 to 23 percent in 1993-1994 (Breneman and Finney 1997). Likewise, state and federal funds to support discoveries and inventions has fallen. This decline is the main factor driving universities to exploit nontraditional revenue sources. And yet large elements of the general public and state legislatures continue to subscribe to the old principle and thus find unfairness.

As universities, and particularly public research universities, consider protective mechanisms to meet the challenges posed by the quest for nontraditional income sources, they would do well to reflect on the unique governance of the university. In this connection, one might view the university as a consortium of four stakeholders—three guilds composed of governing board, faculty, and a conglomerate of students, government, and public, and a bureaucracy that administers the university. Each group differs in knowledge, experience, commitment, stakes, values, and length of association. Interactions among them mainly take place by implicit, rather than explicit, legally enforceable contracts. The university administration, composed by and large of technically competent, full-time, academically oriented managers (bureaucrats?), tends to dominate the quest for nontraditional funds. Their tenure and stake in the institution and its integrity can differ from those of the faculty whose concern is particularly compelling and positions them as guardians of the academic integrity of the institution.

It is in this setting, for example, that the distribution formula of fees from patented innovations must be considered. They are the fruit of the labor of the institution's best faculty, whose scholarship is enriched by their colleagues and students. Inventions and discoveries are patented and commercialized by technology officers of the university, which funds this office and houses the research. At the same time, not only the university, but the state, and even the nation, benefit from the inventions and discoveries. Income derived from them can be spent to further research and training of tomorrow's scientists.

In the light of these considerations, initiatives to tap unconventional funding sources must balance the concerns of all four stakeholders. Enlightened initiatives are likely to emerge from an effective consultative and at times collaborative process by which administration and faculty jointly develop a university policy with regard to nontraditional funding sources, guidelines for each major income source, and institutionalized collaborative review and oversight.

Fruitful cooperation between the university administration and the faculty, in this as in other matters, is facilitated by the existence of an organized body of the faculty, i.e., the academic senate, and a tradition of shared governance. The partners' modus operandi, time commitment, and likely presence at early contacts with donors and business partners differ greatly because faculty, including the inventor, tend to come late into the picture. Much care must be given, therefore, to early establishing detailed guidelines as to which arrangements are unacceptable; what minimum conditions must be met by donors, business partners, and faculty; and how and when faculty inform the administrators of their outside work. Policies and guidelines, once formulated, should be widely disseminated to the university community, legislators, and the general public.

In addition, there is great merit in creating buffer organizations. They could be given responsibility for business aspects of the commercialization of university-owned intellectual property and for the investment of funds produced by these ventures as well as those obtained from private giving. The first could be in the form of a separate full-service technology corporation and the second of an investment company.

CONCLUSIONS

Mounting large private giving campaigns and developing ways to benefit from the research achievements of faculty have become increasingly important elements in the funding of, in particular, research universities. But it is not merely the search for nonconventional funding sources, particularly corporate funding of research and commercialization of university-owned intellectual property, that has brought universities into the world of commerce. Perhaps equally instrumental has been universities' commitment to disseminate their research results, engage in systematic technology transfer, and, in general, to work with industry for the benefit of society and, especially, for their region. In fulfilling their public service function, universities can help establish and nurture industries, particularly high-tech ones; a likely result are healthy high income employment growth and tax base increases in their region. This beneficial outcome should persuade legislatures to increase government funding of their research universities, so that their pressure to find nontraditional funding sources might be somewhat mitigated.

Reliance by universities on what today are nonconventional funding sources is a fait accompli. This development is likely to spread and grow. Universities are, therefore, well advised to prepare themselves to live with such practices, while preserving their academic integrity.

REFERENCES

Atkinson, R.D. (September 25, 1998). "It Takes Cash to Keep Ideas Flowing," *Los Angeles Times*, B9.

Breneman, D.W. and Finney, J.E. (1997). "The Changing Landscape: Higher Education Finance in the 1990s" in Callan, P.M. and Finney, J.E., eds., *Public and Private Financing of Higher Education*. Phoenix: American Council on Education/The Oryx Press, p. 37.

Chapman, G. (January, 1998). "Will Technology Commercialize Higher Education?," *Los Angeles Times*, D1.

Grassmuck, K. (July 25, 1990). "Universities Efforts to Protect Their Patents Aggressively Result in Complex Legal Skirmishes and, Often, Lucrative Royalties," *Chronicle of Higher Education*, A21.

Gregory, W.D. and Sheahen, T.D. (1991). "Technology Transfer by Spin-off Companies Versus Licensing" in Brett, A.M., Gibson, D.V., and Smilor, R.W., eds. *University Spin-off Companies*. Savage, MD: Rowman and Littlefield, pp. 133–52.

Economist. (September, 1998). "Canada : No Ivory Towers," *The Economist* 46, p. 46.

Hollinger, D.A. (1996). *Science, Jews and Secular Culture: Studies in Mid-Twentieth Century Intellectual History*. Princeton, NJ: Princeton University Press, pp. ix.

Lexington. (March 14, 1998). "Bill Bennett, Frustrated Moralist," *The Economist*.

Matkin, G.W. (1994). "Technological Transfer and Public Policy: Lessons from a Case Study," *Policy Studies Journal*, 22 (2), pp. 372-73.

Markus, J. (February 18, 1998). "Universities and Private Firms Cash in on Faculty Research," *The Associated Press, Daily Bruin*.

Putka, G. (December 12, 1997). "Harvard Endowment Strikes Deal to Buy White River, an Insurance-Service Firm," *Wall Street Journal*, B5.

Science. (March 6, 1998). "U.C., Lilly Ask Supreme Court to Hear Insulin Case," *Science*, 1442.

Shelton, G. (March 30, 1998). "Capital Journal," *Los Angeles Times*, A3.

University of California. (1997). *University of California's Relationships with Industry in Research and Technology Transfer*. Oakland, CA: University of California, pp. 285–95.

CHAPTER 8

Networks and Strategic Alliances within and between Universities and with the Private Sector

Hans J. A. van Ginkel

INTRODUCTION: THE END OF SPLENDID ISOLATION

It has become quite obvious; no one can do it alone anymore. It is even doubtful if that was ever possible. But now there even seems no opportunity to escape the need to cooperate with a large and diverse group of partners. Splendid isolation is now impossible. But how to cooperate? With whom? To achieve what?

Scientists contribute to an extensive body of knowledge that has been constructed over the ages and around the world. More and more knowledge is being produced at an accelerating pace. Estimates say the amount of knowledge now doubles every five years. As a consequence, the shelf life of knowledge is declining rapidly. Accordingly, the costs of research have to be recovered in ever shorter time periods.

Modern information and communication technology has arrived just in time to cope with this impressive explosion of knowledge creation and sharing. State-of-the-art information and communications technology already contributes decisively to this process. Informing and sharing, however, is one thing; active cooperation and partnership, another.

This chapter will be about cooperation and partnership, about creating conditions that can bring together persons from different backgrounds and affiliations and, through them, their departments, institutions, or companies. This chapter will also be about conditions that can facilitate new and innovative combinations of disciplinary knowledge and specialists, and that can facilitate knowledge transfer from universities to the private sector, from the industrialized world to developing countries.

GLOBALIZATION AND THE KNOWLEDGE SOCIETY

The processes of globalization and development of the "knowledge society" seem to be closely interlinked. One of the consequences is a rising dominance of market-oriented approaches to organizing and providing education and information services worldwide. Research and higher education are becoming much more utilitarian and their effectiveness is assessed on the grounds of their ability to provide effectively relevant information and skills for dealing with specific tasks. This situation places a greater pressure on the research and higher education systems to be responsive to the perceived needs of the society it seeks to serve. This trend was clearly reflected in the Memorandum on Higher Education, which was presented by the EU Commission in 1991.

Indicative of the type of resistance against such a development was the fact that this memorandum was *not* adopted by the national governments of the member countries because education—including higher education—was and is still seen as an important element in their policies regarding culture and national identity. However, this principle notwithstanding, the views expressed in the EU memorandum have since been introduced in many policy papers at the national level within and outside EU countries.

Universities are asking how their creative and innovative roles can be maintained under these new, rapidly evolving conditions. Higher education has increasingly become a regular part of the education career of the younger generations. When policy papers in the U.S. and France aim at participation rates of 80 percent of an age cohort, this goal clearly relates more to tertiary education than to higher education. How much creativity and innovation can a society or one generation really cope with? How fast can we change? Why should we change, and in which areas?

Higher education has become a big sector in public life. Its sheer size already demands differentiation: division of tasks, division of functional links, different patterns of cooperation, and, related to all this, different internal functional structures, communications, and cooperation patterns. Multi-faceted delivery systems in higher education and research are emerging, challenging the monolithic system dominated by universities and expanding the scope of services and competition within the industry.

We can already observe the emergence of such specialist higher education institutions as research networks and centers that perform tasks once considered the preserve of do-it-all universities. This development is further amplified by more cost-effective electronic communication that gives reality to "virtual universities" and to global networks of research and knowledge exchange without national or regional boundaries.

How to realize "economies of scale" in terms of costs or quality while at the same time preserving challenging working conditions and managing diversity is one of the major challenges universities are currently facing. With the increasing knowledge-intensity of society and the higher demands put on universities, the need to cut costs while at the same time investing in essential, ever more expensive infrastructure, the universities have entered a period of cut-throat competition and selection. This competition requires a strengthening of the synergy within the institution and strategic coalition formation. Universities are confronted with several challenges: to build on existing strengths, using available quality in terms of academics and infrastructure; to create new product–market combinations while at the same time preserving the cultural role of the university and strengthening its ethical and critical contributions.

Neither the traditional academic "noninterference" approach, nor any "let one hundred flowers bloom" strategy will be of use here. Instead, strategies are needed that invite contribution, create synergy, and cooperate with respected, functional partners within and outside the institution. When we take a closer look, universities are seen to be much less different from (bigger) companies in the private sector than many academics prefer to believe.

WHAT CAN WE LEARN FROM THE PRIVATE SECTOR?

When we look at the private sector, we can distinguish a variety of patterns in cooperation generally linked to the different aims of the cooperating corporations. Patterns of "horizontal" cooperation occur when corporations within one industry branch work together in collective wage bargaining with trade unions, in negotiating collective insurance arrangements, in setting common standards on quality, in lobbying, or in doing collective (pre-competitive) research. For instance, in the last decade, the Netherlands' Association of Universities (VSNU) clearly went in that direction. At present, it sees itself as an employers union.

In patterns of "vertical" cooperation, partners from different branches act as suppliers or consultants. These patterns have become increasingly important since the "big is beautiful" ideology has been superseded by the "small is beautiful" approach and eventually by concepts that try to combine the advantages of big organizations with those of smaller scale working environments.

This development has led to mergers in which the original corporations keep their identity (and brand names) and continue to function largely as separate units (e.g., Heineken and Brands Bier, Paccard with DAF-trucks and

British Leyland, and Daimler Benz and Chrysler). Corporations have also been led to reconsider their organization and structure to get back to their "core business," to split off useful but different activities, and to outsource specific tasks. Such developments are no longer a shock to a world that has grown accustomed to middle-class Volvo cars with Renault engines and Mitsubishis coming from a Volvo factory in the Netherlands. This type of development is also not unknown in the world of higher education. In the Netherlands, all the major polytechnics are the result of mergers on the basis of geographical and functional arguments. In France, the *"pôles universitaires"* have tried to mend the harm done by the splitting up along disciplinary and ideological lines of many of the existing universities after the cultural revolution of the late 1960s. The World Bank supports a project in Hungary to merge the many sectorial universities of often very different quality levels into large regional universities.

Such a cooperation pattern can be developed in different ways. Sometimes these have a strongly *hierarchical* nature, e.g., where a multinational company prescribes production and quality standards and even prices to suppliers. These patterns, however, can also be of a more *coordinative* nature, e.g., in cases in which two competing companies set up a joint research program or agree to accept the same standard for new products. The successes and failures that have occurred in research programs and in setting standards in advanced consumer electronics between all relevant corporations, such as Mitsubishi, Sony, and Philips, form a good illustration of the opportunities and difficulties in this area.

In the world of professional sports, the same patterns are developing. Even in higher education, these same patterns appear when, for instance, universities develop strong links with the best secondary schools to ensure both volume and quality of the new groups of students. This cooperation can involve teacher training, curriculum development, or education research. Comparable patterns can develop between medical faculties and hospitals and general practitioners in the region, or between engineering faculties and industries.

CREATING EUROPE: ROLE AND STRATEGIES OF HIGHER EDUCATION

In the development of European Union education, higher education has played a pivotal role from early on. In fact, there seems to be a paradox in the way in which regional governments regard higher education from one side as a topic of primarily national interest, and at the same time use it to prepare the European citizen of tomorrow. Of course, these two points can be reconciled on the basis of the shared vision of a culturally diverse Europe, which sees and exploits its cultural diversity as one of its strengths. Student mobility and the implementation of this vision through a growing number of networks serve the aim of educating a new generation that understands and supports this vision of the richness of cultural diversity.

The Erasmus-Interuniversity Cooperation Projects (ICPs) and the Tempus Joint European Projects (JEPs) have proved to be most successful in this respect. These EU programs were organized largely via discipline-oriented networks. Thus, institutional participation in the programs required member-ship by the individual universities in many disciplinary networks, sometimes over 100.

Although formally the institutions were members—the rector or president had to sign—in practice the departments, or even individual professors, were the aim of these networks. It was often not more than the organization of student mobility. The Tempus program, however, envisaged a broader coop-eration between EU universities and universities in Central and Eastern Europe.

In the world of research, EU funding has often stimulated the development of small international networks. Their aim is to conduct research on a well-defined topic during a specified period of time. These networks seem to be more sustainable than the ICPs, probably because they are run by the research-ers primarily for their own benefit.

The EU explicitly aimed at cooperation beyond the universities in the form of international training partnerships of universities and enterprises. The EU Comett Program stimulated such partnerships on a sectorial (disciplinary) basis or sometimes also on a regional one. This program was much less successful, primarily because of the added difficulty of involving industries. Now the Comett Program has ended.

The universities, however, have not only responded to EU initiatives. Gradually, they have understood the importance of cooperation, across the borders, in education, research, and even public service. Now that the new generation of EU programs defines completely different rules than the earlier programs, in particular in universities participating in their "own" networks, the programs have shown surprising flexibility and adaptability. Europe now has a series of strong, sometimes extensive, institutional networks, e.g., the Coimbra Group, the Santander Group, UNICA, and the Utrecht Network. In engineering and agriculture, strong thematic networks (CAESAR and NATURA) also have been developed.

UNIVERSITIES IN COOPERATION: ENVIRONMENT AND "INVIRONMENT"

Linking universities' competencies to the needs of society not only means that we have to cooperate more with other universities and participate in networks with external partners, it also means that networks work with external partners, and that we have to change our internal organizational structure to be able to work together with partners from different cultures, e.g., universities in other countries, governments (local, regional, national) and their semi-autonomous agencies, and the private sector. Because life itself is not divided into disciplines, departments, or faculties, our partners in society and the business community will often demand answers to questions that have far more dimensions than one discipline can cope with. Besides, most scientific breakthroughs nowadays appear on the interfaces of two or more disciplines. This means that our universities cannot rely on their traditional academic organization only, an organization that in itself can already be questioned because it is so different from country to country and university to university. We must build matrix organizations wherein the disciplines meet in various combinations, different at different times, to cope with such complex issues as sustainable growth, the quality of human life, and the cohesion of societies.

But not only the "environment" demands interdisciplinary cooperation, nowadays researchers within one discipline look more and more over their "fence" to use paradigms of other research fields to overcome the obstacles they encounter within the paradigms of their own discipline. Do we not often read about the evolutionary model, familiar in biological science, as an inspiring source to gain insight into complex sociological problems, or about communication and information technologies when trying to explain the function of DNA? So the "invironment" also seeks new combinations of disciplines to innovate and break through the old paradigms.

The "coordinating capacity" of the institution is then the crucial factor: Who can oversee the various scientific disciplines that change agents within departments, the emerging bright young academics, or the new topics? Who can link the outside network with the inside matrix, the environment with the invironment?

Within the university, research institutes and schools that provide a certain thematic coherence between different disciplines appear to be important organizational tools for the interaction with the environment. As temporary structures (in fact any structure like a center or a task force appears to be helpful) between established departments and faculties, they bring innovation and external orientation without abandoning the disciplinary "roots" of their research and education. Between universities, they offer clear objectives in the form of research and educational programs in which every university can participate with projects and research groups that excel in their field. Between universities and industry/government, they offer programs that seek interdisciplinary answers to complex demands from society.

REGIONAL, NATIONAL, AND GLOBAL PATTERNS OF COOPERATION

A chessboard with more than two dimensions then emerges. We work together in disciplinary and problem-oriented programs with many partners, both within our university and in the outside world at the regional, national, and global levels.

Some parts of our universities participate in networks to exchange Ph.D. students. Others work together with industry to find new medicines. Some groups work together with European universities to solve issues in urban and housing research, while at the same time working with government-funded research institutes to develop a new concept for compact cities and the reduction of automobility. Many networks exist at different scale-levels, interlinked through nodes at different hierarchical levels.

Again, the self-organizing and coordinative power in a university is crucial to be able to play this interesting game of multidimensional chess. One of the ways to get a grip on these networks is to make them part of the university strategy. This means, of course, that universities can make a choice in which networks they want to participate.

Certain networks are crucial for the strategy of the university. For example, many of our universities are faced with decreasing state funding as a consequence of strategies to balance the state budget. If we do not want to compromise our ambitions and objectives, we have to pull away from the traditional overly strong dependency on state funding and gain more financial autonomy. Those networks that enable us, through cooperation with partners in the private sector, to find additional resources must have a high priority in our strategy.

For another example, if a university wants to excel in a certain field of research within an international context, finding highly prestigious, excellent partners to work with has to be its first priority. To be able to find such partners is the strongest recognition a university can obtain.

In the strategic development of its cooperation patterns, the university will have to strive for efficiency and effectiveness. To make work with work, to make double or even triple use of the same work, is a golden rule. The sustainability of the cooperation is another important ingredient for efficiency. Long-term commitment means more in terms of willingness and real cooperation than a short-term contract. Such cooperation and commitment becomes even more concrete when these are materialized in specific, even bilateral, agreements between a few partners only. Strategic alliance is a concept that has proved, at least to Utrecht University, very helpful in creating stronger commitments.

Reflecting on the interactive, long-term, multi-dimensional perspective just discussed, we can see that the traditional concepts of contract research (or education) do not easily apply to the type of external cooperation that is needed, such as agreement on long-term objectives, commitments, mutual investments, and quality of processes, and on how to make an exit. In this type of cooperation, the relationship no longer has the characteristics of a transaction or market contract but of an organization (much like a joint venture). In the first year after this policy was introduced, Utrecht University was successful or lucky enough to conclude strategic alliances with two large, innovative international pharmaceutical companies. In the next year, alliances were formed with a transnational in consumer electronics and medical equipment and a national ministry. A major advantage of the long duration (8 to 10 years) of the alliance and the loose formulation of the objectives is that such alliances are much more compatible with fundamental/basic research than was the regular contract research.

CONCLUSION: DYNAMIC PATTERNS OF ORGANIZATION AND COOPERATION

The foregoing discussion shows that patterns of cooperation have become very diverse and dynamic, depending on the state of the organization, what is inside or outside, how it is organized, and what cooperation can be interchangeable and, indeed, changes over time. What is important, however, is to have a clear idea of the core business and the ways in which this can be furthered by strategic development of functional structures and relations. In this, we can still learn much from practices developed in the private sector. In Europe, the EU has greatly stimulated this process by its programs in higher education and research.

REFERENCE

European Union Commission. (1991). *Memorandum on Higher Education*. Brussels: European Union.

CHAPTER 9

The Research University's Potential as an Area's Growth and Prosperity Stimulant

Peter Preuss

BENEFICIAL EFFECTS OF A UNIVERSITY ON THE ECONOMY

The very presence of a college or a university has a beneficial effect on its surrounding community and region. Moreover, the economic effects of a research university or universities can be especially significant, as can be seen in California's Silicon Valley.

When University of California President Dr. Richard Atkinson was director of the U.S. National Science Foundation, he commissioned a study of the impact of research on the economy. The economists writing the report coined the name "new growth theory," and showed that research is the number one creator of an expanded economy and job growth. Simply stated, they assigned central importance to science and technology-based innovation as factors accounting for 50 percent of this nation's economic growth and its international competitive position.

The U.S. Small Business Administration goes even further. It notes that while major U.S. companies were "downsizing," small businesses were expanding. In the past eight years, they have hired more people than the big companies have let go and are the major factor in the reduction of unemployment in the United States (Glover 1998).

The innovative, high-tech culture in Silicon Valley was born when the communications lab of Stanford University Dean of Engineering Dr. Frederick Terman became the focal point of brilliant engineers, like William Hewlett and David Packard, founders of Hewlett Packard in 1939. Terman maintained many contacts with the business community and acted as a one-man network, introducing his engineers to other engineers, businessmen, professional service providers, and others. Encouraged by the Hewlett Packard success, many other Terman engineers created companies. The Silicon Valley miracle had begun.

Later, Dr. William Shockley, a Nobel laureate and co-inventor of the transistor, left Bell Labs and returned to his boyhood home, Santa Clara County, to found Shockley Laboratories (Malone 1985). Chosen by him partly for its proximity to Stanford University, Shockley Labs quickly spun-out most of the fabled semiconductor industry, including Intel, National Semiconductor, and many others.

The San Francisco Bay Area, comprising nine counties, is now home to 7 million people, has a gross domestic product exceeding $200 billion annually, supports 4,000 high-tech companies employing more than 200,000 people, including 509 bioscience and medical device companies, and is home to the University of California, Berkeley; U.C. San Francisco; U.C. Santa Cruz; U.C. Davis; Stanford University; and Santa Clara University. There is no doubt that Stanford University and the legacy of Frederick Terman is the reason Silicon Valley is where it is!

A research university can help generate jobs, particularly if it is committed, in addition to educating students, to reaching out to private high-tech industries and effectively supporting their undertakings. Such outreach programs can have many dimensions and can be pursued with different degrees of commitment and intensity.

A number of university programs help stimulate innovation and technology. For example, the University of Texas IC^2 (the Institute for Innovation, Creativity and Capital), founded by the legendary entrepreneur George Kozmetsky, teaches courses and publishes books and reports on innovation and entrepreneurship. It has an incubator for new companies. Under its new director, Robert Ronstadt, it plans to reach out to provide more "networking" with the local high-tech business community.

The Minneapolis-St. Paul region of Minnesota, because of the University of Minnesota; Seattle, Washington, because of the University of Washington; and Research Triangle Park, because of Duke University and the University of North Carolina, are also fertile fields for high-tech companies, but have no active university/small business networking organization.

I don't claim that university outreach programs are absolutely essential for economic development, but only that they can enhance the university presence. Beyond the university's physical presence, outreach programs can make a research university the incubator and seedbed of exciting new products and processes so crucial to high-tech firms and their development. With the objective of stimulating economic development and facilitating the creation of new high-tech firms and the growth of existing ones, the university can help develop partnerships of high-tech companies in the region by encouraging fruitful cooperation between them and the university. This objective can be achieved when, for example, an arm of the university assumes some of the following functions:

1. It collects relevant business information about existing firms in the region and widely disseminates it.
2. It sponsors conferences, lectures, and colloquia in which up-to-date high-tech information is imparted.
3. It assists start-up companies in finding funds.
4. It helps build effective networks for members of the high-tech industry.
5. It educates the community and its elected officials on the needs of its growing companies.

THE CONNECT PROGRAM

An example is the CONNECT Program at the University of California at San Diego. The university has determined that business development is a desirable goal and has encouraged the program to do all of the above and also help its industrial members locate and recruit well-trained high-tech engineers. UCSD CONNECT, founded in 1986 by then UCSD Chancellor Richard Atkinson and Associate Vice-Chancellor Mary Walshok, now has over 600 member companies. High-tech companies that have participated in CONNECT events have raised over $5 billion in equity capital, much of which has benefitted the local community. In San Diego, CONNECT has become a catalyst and a recognized benefactor of the community. Clearly a CONNECT-like organization centered at a university can make that university the hub of economic activity.

UCSD CONNECT, under the enthusiastic direction of Bill Otterson, has a staff of 15. Its primary strategy is the creation of events that have strong community participation. It organizes over 60 separate events each year, more than one a week. These events are the networking opportunities that start the system working.

CONNECT's Springboard provides early mentoring by experts to start-up firms by preparing a young researcher or entrepreneur to present their concept for an existing or planned new company to a panel of approximately 10 experts, including CEOs and management from related industry, CPAs, lawyers, patent experts, and technologists. The feedback is specific and tough.

As the company matures, there comes a time when funds from friends, family, and lines of credit are not sufficient. CONNECT's Financial Forum brings in 100 venture capitalists each year to review business plans from emerging companies. Months before the event, a community of local service providers meets to identify the best and most ready company for venture capital. Typically, 60 to 70 companies apply for the event, and the committee selects the best 35. The committee then works with the 35 companies to ensure the quality and clarity of each one's presentation.

Each November, Corporate Partnership Forum brings many of the world's largest pharmaceutical and device companies to San Diego to hear presentations from biotech and medical device companies seeking corporate investments. Again, a UCSD CONNECT committee identifies the potential presenters, selects the best, and coaches the CEOs to present their partnering opportunities in the best light.

The annual Most Innovative New Products Award luncheon celebrates innovation among all local companies in the marketplace. Once again, a committee is organized to identify the best new products in a number of categories, select the finalists, and then to have a big celebration to honor the best products.

Another way of marketing what is going on in the region is the annual UCSD CONNECT directory of members and sponsors. CONNECT now has over 600 sponsors and members, and the directory gives each entity and the university a page to describe their business. The directory conveys the commitment of San Diego to the technology businesses and is the best source of information on technology companies.

CONNECT's Athena program is designed for women high-tech executives. It offers them a networking forum. Its programs meet the special needs of this important and growing group.

To help ensure that UCSD CONNECT meets the needs of industry and the university, it has two advisory boards. The UCSD CONNECT Advisory Board includes CEOs, three science deans from UCSD, venture capitalists, and senior managers from its service providers. The Scientific Advisory Board was formed to help find ways to expand relationships with the university and industry.

The Success of CONNECT

The following elements are the keys to the success of CONNECT:

1. Involving a major research university to provide the technology and the educated workforce.
2. Focusing on economic growth and community service.
3. Giving the customer (industry) what he or she needs—not necessarily what the university needs.
4. Developing a culture that is conducive to entrepreneurs.
5. Involving businesses and their suppliers—establishing the CONNECT community.

6. Working with everyone—excluding no organization or person who wants to participate.
7. Having a committed, entrepreneurial leader.

In addition to such a comprehensive outreach effort, more specific ones can play a major role in assisting the region's high-tech industries. As a consequence, the region's quality of employment opportunities and general prosperity will increase. Individual faculty members or teams that can include members of all institutions in the region can monitor such efforts. What any and all of these efforts have as their common goal is to assist (1) the founding of high-tech start-up companies and (2) the growth of existing ones, through both new and improved products and processes. Graduates who have learned state-of-the-art processes, techniques, or products in undergraduate or graduate school create most start-ups around a major research university.

Either fundamental or applied research results can also be transferred to private firms for commercial exploitation. The transfer can take a number of forms.

1. A faculty member can found a company that commercially uses the new knowledge or material he or she created as a faculty member.
2. The university can patent the new product or process and license it to a private firm.
3. The university can use the patent by joining a private firm in making commercial use of it, possibly founding a start-up company.
4. The university can by itself form a start-up company and make commercial use of the license.

In any of the above technology transfer initiatives, a major contribution is obviously made by the university's conventional teaching and training programs, including those tailored for executives, finance officers, and legal counsel.

Universities, in their historical role as learning communities created to teach, carry out research, and engage in public service, have been held as important to the well-being of society. In turn, society has supported the universities by contributing to their finances. Such an unwritten social contract has existed for sometime.

For various reasons in the recent past, government funding has been declining, putting at risk the ability of universities to fulfil their mission to their fullest capacity. One result could be a declining ability to create new knowledge, expert professional skills, and the ability to serve as technology transfer agents.

As research universities reach out to the community by more directly assisting in the creation and growth of high-tech companies, quality employment grows and prosperity increases. The region's private sector benefits, and so does the public sector. As employment and income in the region's jurisdictions grow, so do their tax receipts. In terms of the social contract between a state's population and its public universities, funding of research universities deserves to once again become more generous.

In this example, the university has a dual role. On the one hand, it helps generate industries, which then need well-educated employees. On the other, it produces the qualified graduates to fill these jobs.

CONCLUSION

Listed below are some of the advantages of outreach programs to the research university itself.

1. Such programs build a dedicated group of commercial supporters for the university.
2. Students may have opportunities for part-time jobs or internships.
3. Faculty may have opportunities for consulting.
4. Faculty may learn new and innovative techniques from industry that can enhance their research.
5. Successful entrepreneurs often return gifts to the university in the form of underwritten chairs, named buildings, etc.

To conclude, I would again like to quote from a speech given by U.C. President Richard Atkinson (1996) to the California Coalition for Science and Technology Summit.

> In opening this conference, I have only three messages. One is that we are living in one of the most exciting periods of intellectual discovery in history, and the economic potential of the explosion of knowledge is tremendous. Another is that we need to be much more active than we currently are in promoting industry-university partnerships in research. And the third is that we must organize ourselves in new ways if we hope to succeed in tapping the productive power of new knowledge to drive the California economy.

REFERENCES

Atkinson, R. (1996). Conference address to the California Coalition for Science & Technology Summit, May 28, Sacramento, California.

Glover, J. (October, 1998). "Mergers and Acquisitions in the United States, 1990-1994," U.S. Small Business Administration.

Malone, M. (1985). The Big Score. New York: Doubleday & Company, Inc., pp. 68–71.

CHAPTER 10

Research and Education
New Roles, New Instruments

Dennis Tsichritzis

INTRODUCTION

U niversities were organized and have developed over the years according to a few valuable principles. Nothing epitomizes these principles better than two simple statements outlined by Wilhelm von Humbold in the last century. The first states that research and education (*Forschung und Lehre*) should be indivisible. Research brings competence and enthusiasm to education, and education brings new people and fresh ideas to research. The second statement emphasizes the environment of solitude and freedom (*Einsamkeit und Freiheit*) that should prevail in universities. Solitude protects academics from unwarranted outside pressures, and freedom allows their natural curiosity and creativity to develop. These four qualities have served the university well over the years and have guided the establishment of universities as we know them today. Solitude influenced the development of the university campus, for example. Freedom encouraged the award of tenure and the management structure of the university. Research demanded the establishment of research institutes and programs and is the guiding force in the programs of both undergraduate and graduate schools.

There is no reason to question or discard principles that have served the university so well over the centuries. Indeed, they are at the center of the social contract between the university and its environment. We should, however, periodically reevaluate our goals and adapt the principles to our new world. This reevaluation is happening now and it is being forced upon us by intellectual, economic, and political changes.

Universities are part of a general knowledge society that is expanding at an increasingly greater pace. The value of this knowledge is no mere abstraction. Knowledge is a critical renewable resource. Producing, packaging, and distributing knowledge are important businesses. Universities cannot remain unchanged if they hope to play a central role in an important and fast changing economic activity. They need to adapt their goals, their structure, and their instruments.

RESEARCH AND INNOVATION

Traditionally, research in universities is fundamental, open, and free. It is fundamental insofar as academics are admired and rewarded when they discover new areas or solve well-known problems. The librarian's citation index rewards the initiators of a research topic, but nothing is considered so valuable as to shed light on an issue that others have tried for years or centuries to resolve. Research in universities is open to the extent that publications are still considered the main measure of success. An academic career is supposed to advance continuously with a couple of publications per year. Promotion, tenure, and status are related to publications. Finally, research in universities is free from the intrusions of management. Each professor and each researcher is supposed to decide freely where and when he or she is committing his or her brain cycles. Freedom is considered an essential aspect of creativity. The drive and the impulses to succeed are supposed to come from within. Researchers who cannot define their research agendas and have a limited spirit of independence are considered second rate.

Research is not intended to be a sterile intellectual pastime. It is supposed to have an end. It is supposed to create new knowledge, to clarify, and to innovate. The results of this innovation process, the new ideas, are transmitted through two channels. The first is publication. Publication is not a goal in itself. It is a communication conduit to other contemporary or future researchers. The second channel is through the heads of students. Students, especially graduate students, participate in research projects and transmit new knowledge wherever they go. The pressure on students to change institutions or to go into industry helps transmit many more ideas and experiences, most of which cannot be captured by publication alone.

This research environment, which evolved over the years in universities, is entrenched in structures, in procedures, and, most important, in the mentalities of the persons involved. However, two developments create difficulties. First, research results and the potential applications of innovation are becoming valuable in economic terms. The economic interests are so enormous that they distort the whole picture. Second, the timeframes are becoming shorter. Research results have to be promoted immediately or they lose their value. These two new developments create a very competitive and dynamic research market. It is questionable whether universities can effectively compete in this market with their old framework.

THE RESEARCH MARKET

It is not unusual for successful companies to obtain more than 50 percent of their earnings from products that were not around five years ago. This trend implies that companies are forced by the market to package new products at an ever increasing pace. Innovation is becoming a strategic advantage more important than cost cutting or financial strength. Especially in high-tech areas, such as information technology, a company's very existence can be in danger if it misses a few important innovations.

Companies once had separate research laboratories and divisions that were operating rather like universities, although the work was less fundamental, less open, and more controlled. The hope was that these research centers, if you will, could be directed to work on significant problems for the future development of the company. In addition, company research was doing technology tracking, following developments in other research laboratories. Finally, companies would often have pools of experts to draw upon in task forces to help guide management and give valuable consulting to the operating divisions.

This model of semi-academic research for companies is becoming obsolete. First, the cost of the research division is considerable, and management questions it under the pressure of shareholder value. Second, it is difficult to direct research according to the company needs. Third, technology transfer between research and operating divisions is always problematic. Finally, research often produces results that are valuable but incompatible with company strategy.

Companies are responding by phasing out, distributing, or co-opting their research divisions. Phasing out means slowly reducing and redistributing the staff. Distributing means moving research groups directly to the operating divisions. Co-opting means that operating divisions participate in the financing and management of research. All these solutions acknowledge indirectly that a company's innovation strategy is too important to rest solely on the research division. Companies increasingly obtain the innovation they need directly from outside. There are many different ways for a company to buy innovation. It can outsource research projects. It can participate in research projects or in consortia with specific goals. It can buy or exchange innovation from other companies in the form of patents and licenses. It can merge with or buy out other companies. It can participate in the capital of other companies.

Finally, it can run its own venture capital operations, spinning off companies or encouraging start ups. All these operations create a large research and innovation market.

Universities offering only traditional research find it hard to participate in this market. They have a dual problem. First, they need to aggressively promote themselves and their results in this market. Second, they need to collect the benefits due to them from this market. In many universities, both operations are difficult. Academics are not necessarily the best marketing persons. Some of them consider marketing to be contrary to scientific valor. Others are interested in promoting themselves and their personal interests and not necessarily the university's interests. In addition, university administrations, although excellent in controlling spending, are not necessarily good in obtaining money from the research market.

Some universities have learned that research cannot just be given away when people knock on the door. They run technology-transfer operations, patent offices, techno-parks, and the like. They sign contracts with companies, they reserve exploitation rights, they charge overheads on research projects, and they finance staff with soft money. All these are potential instruments. There is, however, an important policy question. To what extent should a university enter the innovation market, and how? To be sure, universities should move decisively and aggressively in the research market; they cannot afford to stay out. The research market is and will continue to be very lucrative. Universities outside this market will find it impossible to finance academic activities or obtain top people. Slowly, there will be a concentration of top talent where the best financial and infrastructural conditions exist. The rest of the universities will slowly drift downward to the level of the community college. Even universities with large endowment funds, or strong alumni associations, or strong historical roots, or good political support will find it hard to compete. The research market will eventually designate winners and losers. One sees already the first signs of companies concentrating their attention and their financing on universities that best fit their interests.

COMPETENCE CENTERS

Universities cannot effectively compete with innovation-centered companies (the universities' real competitors) in a research market by only adapting their traditional structures. A technology transfer office and a couple of lawyers and marketing people are not enough. They have to develop special structures that operate practically as separate companies. We propose a structure of competence centers.

A university competence center should be thought of as a separate company wholly owned, or at least controlled, by the university with many other potential industrial partners. It should be managed as a company with clear goals and a business plan. Its staff can be shared with the university but staff members would have other responsibilities and other roles while working in the center. A competence center would survive in business terms only for as long as it can obtain sufficient funds. The university plays a role as a holding company relative to its competence centers. It launches them, closes them, or carries them over in times of need.

A competence center does all the things that academic research is allergic to. It contacts companies, builds prototypes, runs certification, sells patents and licenses, creates spin-offs, and runs industrial labs. It has a small number of more permanent staff, the rest being on short-term contracts. It operates as a small-sized (100–150 persons) innovation company. It feeds on the academic research and produces results for the innovation market.

Competence centers are not aligned according to academic faculties. They combine disciplines as they are needed by the innovation market. Not every faculty needs a center, and centers may combine talents coming from different faculties or departments.

A competence center cannot operate on a profit basis without some subsidies. A reasonable mix is 50/50 between institutional funding and resources coming from outside. The 50 percent institutional funding may come from the university (perhaps as people's time, as buildings, or as infrastructure); from local, regional, and national government; and from some large sponsors. The other 50 percent may be obtained through contracts, small or large, short or long, depending on the business plan.

Competence centers tie the university to the economic activity and allow it to be very visible in specific areas. In addition, they indirectly provide a great environment for training students. Finally, competence centers have a pool of practical talent that can be used for education or training for the rest of the university. Most universities already run such a competence center, albeit for special purposes, such as a university hospital.

EDUCATION AS STORYTELLING

Teaching and learning form a complicated process of minds coming together and exchanging knowledge. We will not even attempt to discuss here the fine details of such an environment. However, two components of the process stand out. First, storytelling is an important component of teaching in that it describes in abstract but vivid terms what needs to be learned. Second, experience-gathering is an equally important component that brings more concrete and direct evidence to the subject. In this section, we will discuss storytelling and in the next section experience-gathering.

Storytelling goes back to the beginning of knowledge transfer. One can visualize a group of people listening to somebody explaining what he knew, followed by a discussion on clarifications. No infrastructure or learning method was needed except a common language.

Storytelling evolved over the years and eventually became ex-cathedra lecturing, such as we observe today in universities. The fact that blackboards have yielded today to transparencies, slides, and PowerPoint images does not imply any great change. On the contrary, part of the interaction was lost as the groups became larger and the lectures more formal. Storytelling is assisted by written documents, and by the library as a place for individual learning and contemplation.

When looking back at storytelling in areas outside education, we see a dramatic change. New technologies appeared and changed storytelling in film, television, CD-ROMs, Web TV, and the like. Still, education remained untouched, apart from an ill-fated attempt to introduce television. In many universities lecturing goes on as before, while computers are used to prepare the overheads.

We believe that education via storytelling will change dramatically over the next few years. This change is practically feasible and economically inevitable for a number of reasons. First, the technology is here, is affordable, and is easy to use. From the Web to multimedia, we see a new generation of tools that are widely available and cheap. Second, content is becoming more widely available by the day. Some of it is of good quality, and its range and applicability will increase. Third, a new generation of university teachers knows how to use multimedia and pump the Internet for information. Finally, students are becoming computer-literate, and expect lectures to be exciting and up-to-date.

How will all this affect university lecturing? First, book libraries will gradually be replaced by all-encompassing digital libraries available on the networks. Libraries will be there, but they will play a limited role as rare document collections. Most people will not need to consult the real thing. Second, students will have access to too much information. They will come to lectures to be motivated and to interact with other people. Professors will need to be mentors rather than explainers. Third, much content will be available for import. Lengthy stylized explanations need not be repeated. They will be available on demand. Fourth, experts will become available on demand through telepresence to enhance the experience and bring new elements into the discussion. Fifth, interactions will increase. Most students will come to a lecture mainly to interact. The lecture will become more of a discussion forum. Finally, many passive spectators may choose to drop in during real time or to examine the event later at their convenience.

In summary, a lecture can become a performance with one moderator, many active participants, packaged material, a script, much spontaneity, a present audience, and a remote and more passive audience. It is storytelling in the best possible tradition. On the other hand, boring repetition of explanations by the same person on material widely available is totally unnecessary. It is the equivalent of monks copying books in an age of printing presses. It will probably become obsolete.

EDUCATION AS EXPERIENCE-GATHERING

Storytelling is not sufficient to transmit knowledge. People need direct verification through experience. In this way, the abstractions, the words, are complemented with personal and direct involvement. Over the years in universities, experience-gathering was also stylized in labs and visits. Labs were able to duplicate real phenomena in small scale, and visits allowed direct contact. We will discuss the ways that these kinds of experiences can be changed or even substituted by using modern technology.

Labs were never the real thing; they were only artifacts representing the real thing. When one performs an experiment it is real, but it is not of the same scale as a natural phenomenon. Two mental exercises are necessary: first, to visualize the phenomenon on the basis of what is measured, and, second, to imagine the phenomenon at its real scale. There is, therefore, some kind of augmented reality with one's imagination.

In visits, one is confronted with a similar experience. Since the visit is short, one doesn't have time to see everything; the rest must be imagined. Moreover, a single glimpse lets many details escape. Part of the abstraction is verifiable but not the details. Again, one has to imagine both the details and the invisible parts to get a whole picture. One augments reality on the basis of the abstractions one knows. This is the reason why a visit to a museum or a city is much more beneficial when one has studied beforehand.

What modern technology offers in terms of virtual reality is the ability to experience phenomena directly and with many senses. In addition, an exciting interactive environment can be installed so that a person can interact in real time and concentrate on a much more personalized tour. In addition, one can superimpose abstraction and augmented reality and play out different hypotheses.

We expect many lab sessions and on-site visits to be partially replaced by augmented reality experiences. We emphasize "partially" because people will always be attracted to real all-encompassing experiences. The huge advantages of this environment are that it can be inexpensive, personalized, repeatable, interactive, and remote. It lends itself to many experiences where visits are impossible or expensive, or where experiments are either destructive or dangerous. The whole environment of education as experience-gathering will be revolutionized with these techniques.

TELELEARNING SERVICES

Technology offers new possibilities in the teaching–learning process. It also opens wide a new market: telelearning services. Telelearning is not new. Special universities have been formed, so-called "free universities," to offer telelearning, first with mail and then with combinations of mail, radio, and television. In addition, many universities are offering continuous education at least regionally and often based on analog video technology.

However, two developments influence this area tremendously. First, globalization has unleashed new competitive pressures. Companies need great competence in their personnel. This, in turn, creates a need for continuous learning on an unprecedented scale. Companies respond in different ways, from renewing their personnel to creating their own internal universities. Clearly, the continuous education market will be large. It is not at all clear how this market will be satisfied. Nor is it clear who will be paying for the retraining: the employees, the companies, or the state?

Universities have always considered continuous education to be a side activity. Professors were not so excited about offering continuous education courses. They often duplicated their normal courses in the evening. The attendees were paying small fees and were not very demanding. Too often they were retired persons eager to fill their time with some intellectual activity. This is far from what is needed today. The potential clients are willing to pay but they expect top quality service. They need courses fitted to their needs, up-to-date and personalized. They also expect perfect organization. In short, they are demanding clients in a competitive market. Universities are often geared to serve captive clients in a monopolistic market. To be a player in the new continuous education market, universities need to change.

The second development is technological. The global availability of the Internet, the availability of broadband networks, the arrival of affordable multi-media PCs, digital TV, and many other technologies create a new environment. The emerging standards provide a stable platform for the production, packaging, and dissemination of content. Companies and institutions are racing to position themselves in this market. The universities have the knowledge workers, but they only have a limited time to react decisively.

There are three aspects of telelearning services: production, packaging, and distribution. Universities can enter any one area or all three. Production of educational content is probably the most lucrative but the most difficult. It needs professional studio techniques, specialized personnel, and high standards. Not every professor can be a television star and not every professor can be schooled to be a great content provider. Putting a camera in a classroom is not content production. We doubt seriously whether universities can enter into content production by themselves. They need alliances. The best is to combine their talent with media producing companies. The resulting units should operate as separate companies with clear business plans. Universities should move quickly—specialized media production companies may not need them forever.

Packaging of content in programs is more accessible. The university uses its reputation and its experience in putting together course modules and in integrating courses into programs. In addition, the award of a certificate or a diploma offers a certification much desired by clients. Successful telelearning packages need to respond to market needs. The university cannot just offer what it has. It will also be wise to input the best quality content, and unrealistic to expect that all the best content can be produced locally.

Finally, distribution of telelearning services uses the regional contents of a university, plus its facilities, its infrastructure, and its personnel as animators. Universities need not distribute their own programs. They can distribute world class programs packaged and produced elsewhere. It sounds radical for a university to distribute a telelearning package with a certificate coming from another university. It is, however, inevitable if the local university does not have something better for the market needs. The separation of telelearning services in production, packaging, and distribution mirrors what has already happened in television. Global players are producing content. Regional players are packaging content in television programs. Local players are distributing the programs.

Universities may choose to enter any of these three sectors. They have to consider possible alliances, to set up proper structures, and to take the matter very seriously. Universities that come late or half heartedly will be pushed out. Once out, universities risk staying out. Universities that think that language or any other legal or artificial barrier will protect them from competitors are wrong. This is a global, competitive business in the same way as film or television. The only way to survive is to compete successfully globally.

NEW ROLES AND STRUCTURES

Over the years, universities have developed a stable structure in terms of schools, faculties, and departments. They have also developed levels for personnel in terms of deans, professors, and associate and assistant professors. Academic research is fitted approximately into the same structure. Research areas correspond to the education structure. In addition, deans are sort of research directors, professors research fellows, associate professors senior researchers, and assistant professors junior researchers.

We see lately that the two directions, education and research, have some difficulties co-existing in the same structure. Research is becoming interdisciplinary and evolves more dynamically. Educational structures are tied with programs and degrees and have difficulty changing. In addition, some professors are great at teaching but mediocre in research, and great researchers often have no interest in teaching. Such difficulties are usually settled in an ad hoc manner to avoid creating separate structures.

If basic education and academic research can somehow co-exist in the same structures, it is not at all the case for competence centers and telelearning services. They both need to respond quickly to markets outside the university, and they cannot survive in the existing structures of the university.

Besides being viewed as separate entities with their own management structure, competence centers should have a strong director, project leaders, and project members. Directors would be term-appointed. Project leaders and project members would be dynamically assigned according to the project mix, and would be on temporary appointments. Tenure makes no sense for such a unit, which is business-oriented and operates according to usual business practices.

Telelearning services should also be organized as business units. Each service relating to a particular economic sector (not academic discipline) should have a strong manager, program supervisors, and course animators. Service managers would be term-appointed. Program supervisors and course animators would be dynamically assigned according to the services offered. Again, tenure does not makes sense, it is a business service unit.

The fact that both competence centers and telelearning services operate in a businesslike fashion outside the structures of the university facilitates running them as alliances with other companies as partners. If these two sectors need to have new structures, it is worthwhile to reconsider also the traditional sectors of basic education and academic research. We would therefore suggest as a mental exercise that academic research be organized outside basic education in a research division with research institutes in only those areas where the university has strong research interests. Research institutes would have research directors with senior and junior researchers as personnel. It is debatable whether any one of these persons needs tenure. Research directors would be term-appointed, and senior and junior researchers would be temporary and assigned on academic research projects.

Why should basic education persons need tenure? For historical reasons perhaps, but there is nothing to distinguish them from the rest of the units. Deans, professors, and junior professors can all be term appointed. Are there any staff that need to be permanent? In the same way as in other service sectors, legal offices, and consulting or financial services, some persons considered as partners need to be tenured. Some deans, research directors, competence center directors, or telelearning service managers can be offered tenure as an acknowledgement of long and valuable service and close identification with the institution.

CONCLUSIONS

Universities were once thought of mainly as places for educating the elite. Research and discovery was an intellectual exercise. The products of this research were freely and widely distributed. Now universities are an important economic actor. They can be leveraged for economic gain both individually and regionally. Universities cannot stay the same when their research by-product (educating people is the main product) becomes a strategic economic advantage.

Universities were once organized for educating young people for a limited time period, say 5 to 10 years. People, however, are increasingly finding that they constantly need an upgrade in their skills during their lifetime. Continuous lifelong learning is becoming a factor forced by globalization and the fast pace of innovation. Continuous learning was once a niche activity for universities. It may take such proportions in the future that university education becomes a niche activity of a vast continuous learning process.

We have outlined many possible changes coming to the university from outside market developments and exciting new technologies. We have proposed the organization of a university in the following four sectors:

1. Basic education with a traditional structure of faculties and departments and traditional levels of authority as deans, professors, and junior professors
2. Academic research with a structure of research institutes with research directors and senior and junior researchers
3. Competence centers with center directors, project leaders, and project members
4. Teleteaching services with service managers, program supervisors, and course animators

Each of the four activities is optional for an institution. One can perhaps have only basic education, as with community colleges. One can have only academic research, as with research centers on fundamental research. One can have only competence centers, as research centers on applied research. Finally, one can have only teleteaching services, as with some free universities or training companies.

An institution can adopt interesting combinations. For example, basic education and teleteaching services, or academic research and competence centers. It can have basic education and academic research, as do most universities. It can have competence centers and telelearning services. Finally, it can have potentially all of them but not necessarily in all scientific areas.

The advantage of combining many sectors among basic education, academic research, competence centers, and teleteaching services is that one can reinforce the other. Reputation in one can help launch the other. People can be shared in different roles in different activities. Finally, people can move between activities, playing different roles at different times. It may, for instance, be advantageous for a person to move from academic research to competence centers or from basic education to telelearning services.

A university cannot and should not enter all activities in all scientific areas. A strict selection is required to position the university. This selection implies that some hard and unpopular decisions have to be made. Whether a university can, with today's management procedures, arrive at such decisions is a different problem. One hopes that it will be discussed in some companion paper on university governance.

Universities developed over the years, combining education and research in a free and isolated environment. Education and research (*Forschung und Lehre*) were served in a perfect solitude and freedom (*Einsamkeit und Freiheit*). We see two new directions coming: market-driven competence centers and telelearning services. Universities must decide if, when, how, and with whom they want to enter these markets. This decision is far more important than using particular technologies to streamline what already exists. Universities cannot for long avoid taking these decisions. Their monopoly as knowledge providers, packagers, and distributors is breaking up on all fronts. Universities should realize that they compete not only with other universities. They are part of a gigantic, lucrative, and extremely competitive knowledge business that is shaping our society. They have to play a strong role if they hope to play any role at all.

CHAPTER 11

Higher Learning as a Joint Venture between State and Industry

The Example of the International University in Germany

Heide Ziegler

ANALYSIS OF THE PRESENT SITUATION

It may well be true that any democratic state has a moral obligation to educate its citizens, and that a fair amount of its taxes should be allotted to this task. It is also true that especially industry and commerce profit from a flourishing system of higher education, and that they should therefore contribute to its success above and beyond tax obligations. However, even democratic states tend to exert a regulatory and sometimes stifling influence on their institutions of higher learning through an increasingly elaborate administrative system—an influence that often hampers necessary development in the areas of research and teaching. At the same time, industry and commerce, although calling for excellent graduates and marketable research results, often neglect to contribute the funds necessary to guarantee the independence of these institutions of higher learning, and to alleviate some of the restrictive measures imposed by the state. Still far from being generally accepted is the insight that optimal results in research and teaching require a measure of controlled independence to be granted to institutions of higher learning. This type of independence can, for instance, be achieved if universities are funded by different parties that are permitted to exert a certain amount of influence on the mission of a university but not allowed to interfere with the methods developed to fulfill that mission.

Interestingly, universities themselves would often rather seek shelter under the roof of the state or—nowadays—large companies and corporations than strive for greater independence. Here the German university system may well be prototypical. German universities tend to be state-funded, although a few private universities exist. Most notable among these are the universities of Eichstätt, funded by the state of Bavaria and in part by the Catholic Church, and Witten-Herdecke, funded by a consortium of companies and foundations, especially the Bertelsmann Stiftung, plus the state of Nordrhein-Westfalen. In contrast to universities in the United States, where tuition fees are charged irrespective of their status as a private or a state institution, German universities at present may not charge tuition fees as long as they continue to be state institutions. The recently elected Social Democratic government may even attempt to pass a federal law against tuition fees, which would be in accordance with their policy, held since the end of the 1960s, when universities were opened up to an increasing number of students. At that time, the moral obligation of the state to educate its citizens was proclaimed a civil right, the Bürgerrecht auf Bildung. Thus the demand for education increased while the universities lost the power to cope with student numbers. As a result, overall standards tended to decline or the duration of studies got longer. Whereas formerly about 5 to 8 percent of the population enrolled at a university after high school graduation, numbers have now risen to 30 percent and are still increasing. None of the Länder in the Federal Republic of Germany, all of which finance their own institutions of higher learning, has been able to meet the ensuing demands for additional buildings, teaching personnel, and equipment. On the contrary, with the possible exception of Bavaria, all German Länder have begun to drastically cut the budget costs for their universities. In Baden-Württemberg, for instance, 10 percent of the universities' teaching and administrative staff will be laid off over the next 10 years. Notable results are the loss of quality in teaching, accompanied by growing student dissatisfaction. It remains to be seen whether students who protest against tuition fees protest against them mainly because they fear the loss of what they have come to see as a civil right or because of the expected small return they would be getting for their money.

German students often do not see their time at a university as preparation for the job market, and due to the present precarious job situation (some areas in Germany, especially in the new Länder, have an unemployment rate of more than 18 percent), students tend not to leave the university, preferring to retain student status, which grants them a number of privileges (cheap health insurance, reduced traffic expenses, inexpensive theater and museum tickets, etc.). These part-time students depreciate the university system even further.

It is fairly obvious then why foreign students, American or Australian, or students from the Pacific Rim, no longer want to study in Germany—a fact that has been lamented over the last couple of years. The language barrier is an additional impediment, making a stay of one or two semesters in Germany appear disadvantageous, especially since programs are too loosely structured for achieving a degree in a calculable period of time.

There are few real incentives to change anything for the better, to reform the universities from within. Because professors and high administrators in the German university system are civil servants—as are all the teachers in primary and secondary schools—all university salaries are devoid of any success-oriented component. Evaluation of teaching, for instance, takes place only randomly, most often only when and if a professor happens to be interested in the opinion of his or her students. Salaries are dependent on age and family status, not on performance. Despite appearances to the contrary, adequate performance is still taken for granted; it is not controlled. Governance in a German university never means control. Every professor—and ideally every student—is free to pursue his or her own goals, both in the areas of research and teaching. Thus, the autonomy of the academic community, and indeed the idea of the academic community itself, is evoked mainly to protect this tradition. Hence the importance attached to "independent" research, and hence also the power of the full professor, whose "assistant" professors are supposed to guarantee his or her independence.

CORPORATE UNIVERSITIES

Strangely enough, at least at first glance, German companies doing business internationally do not seem to be interested in contributing to, and investing in, university education. Instead, they follow the American lead and found their own corporate universities. In 1998, Lufthansa founded the Lufthansa School of Business, Daimler followed suit and founded the Daimler-Benz Corporate University, and Bertelsmann relies on strategic alliances with well-known American business schools, like Harvard, to educate its top managers. All these so-called universities are business oriented, and they clearly function as management training centers. They are top-down institutions and serve the purpose of implementing any change that might occur in the overall mission of the corporation. At the same time, large German corporations are relocating parts of their production, as well as parts of their R&D endeavors, into more cost-effective countries because graduates in those countries are often more eager, younger (therefore less expensive), and more flexible than young German employees.

At best, German firms are still looking for cooperation with universities in some areas of applied research because this kind of cooperation may be very cost-effective. Industry pays for the academic expertise, while often using academic staff and equipment that has already been paid for by the state. Unfortunately, this situation gives rise to the question whether research done in Germany is actually *better* than research conducted, say, in India or in Hong Kong, let alone in the United States (where German companies like Siemens or Daimler invest heavily in university research and development) or whether it is simply *less costly* because it is partly subsidized by the state. Many corporations seem to understand these cooperations with the scientific community as timely but temporary and strictly project-oriented measures. They do not seem to feel that the true capital to be gained by such an investment is human capital, the intelligence of young people devoted to the pursuit of knowledge. True technology transfer, however, consists of the fact that these young people, in furthering their own research, work on a special project that may or may not lead to marketable results. If the education of these young people, however, is not part of the companies' mission, but left to the state in its present "state," then both the academic standard and the devotion of these young people become significantly lower. Such a development has begun to appear in Germany, and the economic recession that accounts for increasing budget cuts in almost every one of the *Länder* is now leading German universities into an existential crisis of both recognition and endowment.

HIGHER LEARNING AS A JOINT VENTURE BETWEEN STATE AND INDUSTRY

Given this situation, Andreas Reuter and I—formerly vice-president and president of the University of Stuttgart, respectively—decided that the German university system needs to be reformed before it loses its high reputation abroad, and that it cannot be reformed from within. We decided that only a private new university, which we called the International University in Germany, could address the issues of a highly developed, yet somewhat stagnant industrial society like Germany, and offer a real solution to a number of problems in the field of higher education, providing that industry and commerce could be induced to see a need for such an institution. For a number of reasons, the university would need to cooperate closely with universities (and companies) in the United States. First and foremost, industry and commerce in the United States have for a long time understood the importance of higher learning as a prerequisite for their own managerial and business success. The alumni programs of American universities are not just a welcome source of the wealth of many universities, but an expression of a mutual understanding that close links need to be maintained between corporations and institutions of higher learning if a country wants to be successful and play a decisive role in the world. At the moment, the United States is the only superpower among nations, but future superpowers like India and China are emerging. For the United States, it is necessary to define and maintain areas of influence, and higher education plays a decisive part in that strategic game. The education of foreign students in the United States provides a higher yield towards the GNP than the export of agricultural products. The American model could teach German policy-makers and industrial magnates that together they need to define the future role of Germany—not only in Europe, but worldwide—in terms of their human capital.

Another reason why the International University in Germany will cooperate with universities in the United States is that in this way it can offer programs of particular interest to companies worldwide. During its initial phase, the International University will focus on two programs, an MBA and a Master of Science in Information and Communication Technology (MICT). The scope and influence of information technology as an applied science has not yet been completely understood even by computer science itself. However, any reform of the German university system would be doomed to failure from the start if it did not take into account the growing importance of how information technology will change our ways of perceiving and coping with the world. For one thing, it will call for other social skills than those prevalent in German universities today. The Humboldtian notion of the isolated individual attempting to attain "objective" truth, alone, almost by virtue of noncommunication, will become obsolete. Today, however, this notion is still very much alive in academia. Learning how to work in groups and teams is seldom considered an end in itself. Research is often conducted in teams, but the areas of teaching and research have been severed to the point where, to the professor, students and their concerns seem to be of secondary importance.

Such is definitely not the case in corporate universities, where the idea of research is not of overriding concern. Corporate universities tend to be business schools, and their end is the better management of the company's income and investments. Corporate universities are not primarily content providers; they are ambitious training programs. Applied research there means research that is already being applied, not research that is conducted with a view of being applied in the future. In Germany, corporate universities are no alternative to the existing state universities. What is needed instead is a new unity of research and teaching to fulfill the contemporary needs of German society. Within a global context, Germany cannot waste energies furthering research or teaching when human capital is what must be invested in.

THE INTERNATIONAL UNIVERSITY IN GERMANY

The International University in Germany addresses these societal needs. It is a private organization that started operating in September 1998. Its purpose is to complement the public system of higher education in Germany by means of its international orientation in research, curriculum, and teaching methods.

We want to stress the role of teaching by moving into an educational field, namely information technology (IT), where research and teaching cannot be legitimately separated. Ideally, an IT-oriented education means that mentors, or facilitators, and students together have to come to grips with problems that cannot now be compartmentalized and departmentalized because we still lack the strategies to organize the data of our information age.

We want to internationalize higher education in Germany. Therefore, we intend to admit 50 percent German and 50 percent non-German students to our university. The common language will be English. Students will work together in teams, particularly during their internships, and they will learn to respect cultural differences by being exposed to another culture. Foreign students will have to learn German and get to know German culture; German students can choose among a variety of other languages and cultures—not all of them European.

Listed below are the principal features of the International University in Germany:

- Classes are completely taught in English. Students are required to learn German as part of their education, but not as a prerequisite for entering the university.
- Although education is based on rigorous scientific standards, there is a strong emphasis on practical experiences via internships, external project work, etc.
- The part of the education that is aimed at acquiring facts and techniques is based on multi-media and teleteaching technology. This technology will enable students to pick the most comprehensive course material for their agenda from a growing number of offerings on the World Wide Web. The resources saved by that approach will be directed toward case-based studies in small groups.
- Students will be strongly encouraged (and supported) to pursue their studies in at least one other university. To this end, the International University in Germany will establish joint curricula with partner institutions worldwide, enabling students to stay on track in respect to their curriculum, while working in different environments and cultures.

- The process of studying is efficiently organized to meet goals within a short time of study. Each year comprises three terms. The bachelor degree has nine terms and the master's another six terms.
- Foreign students enjoy continuous support by German host families, although the students live on their own.
- Initially, two subject areas are being offered for a master's: an International MBA, and a Master of Information and Communication Technology (MICT). The MBA program includes a strong component of IT, while the MICT also offers courses in business administration.

The International University in Germany enjoys strong support from numerous large companies, especially in the high-tech field, such as SAP, IBM, Deutsche Telekom, and Siemens, to mention a few. The state of Baden-Württemberg is also a partner in the joint venture.

Since the International University in Germany is set up as a private enterprise, it is able to operate by other rules than the public universities; there will be, however, a close cooperation between these public universities and the International University in Germany.

The International University in Germany is an attractive option for students who consider an education abroad, but who would normally not choose Germany because of the language problems and because of the long duration of studies in the normal German university system. Moreover, the notion of sharing curricula with partner universities results in a variety of additional options: one can complete part of the curriculum at home, and another part abroad, or one can acquire the bachelor's degree at one (foreign) university, and the master's at another, all in a pre-organized compatible fashion.

Given this and the fact that project work and international internships play a pivotal role in its curricula, it is clear that the International University in Germany implements a scheme that could become a model for university cooperation in a future global education process. The International University attempts to become part of a global network while retaining local links and using German cultural studies and involvement with German companies as an example of how internationally oriented strategies can be anchored in a definable set of values.

CHAPTER 12

Governance

Howard Newby

INTRODUCTION

D
uring the last two or three years, higher education in the U.K. has undergone a severe bout of introspection. Official reports produced on further education, lifelong learning, and work-based learning have culminated in the National Committee of Inquiry into Higher Education, the so-called 1997 Dearing Report. This report covered a wide spectrum of issues in higher education and attempted to plot the course ahead for the sector over the next 20 years. Its recommendations, and implications, are still being digested by all the relevant stakeholders, not least the government.

This spate of reports and inquiries is part of the public process of coming to terms with the shift in the U.K. towards a system of mass higher education. This shift has, of course, been common throughout the Western world in recent years. However, in the U.K., the growth in higher education has been unplanned and, to a large extent, uneven. As little as a decade ago, it was still plausible to describe British higher education as an elite system. As a result, public attitudes towards higher education have tended to lag behind changes in the system itself. Issues still abound about how higher education should be funded, how it should be extended, and even what it is for. As Peter Scott (1995) has remarked, "it is as if we have acquired a mass system in a fit of absentmindedness and have yet properly to exorcise our regrets about the passing of an elite system in which were bounded all that was (apparently) best about British higher education." But however great the sense of bereavement may be—and in some parts of the British higher education system a strong sense of mourning remains—wider socio-economic forces continue to drive the U.K., and most other post-industrial economies, towards the abandonment of the old elite higher education system.

It is not the purpose of this chapter to analyze these forces in detail. A few reminders will suffice. As the most economically advanced nations have moved from "industrial" to "post-industrial" economies, the sources of their economic competitiveness have become increasingly knowledge-based. The quality of human resources and skills is therefore widely regarded as a key element in sustaining economic competitiveness. Furthermore, as markets are becoming increasingly globalized and capital increasingly mobile, so economic success is being regarded as increasingly tied to the flexibility and adaptability of a highly skilled labor force. Changes in the structure of organizations, whether public or private, have also increased the demand for certain kinds of generic skills, while the growing pace of both technological and social change has ushered in an era of lifelong learning, whereby these skills need to be constantly refreshed and updated.

Thus, the quality of demand for higher education is being transformed. Participation has become semi-compulsory for large sections of the population, for to be a nongraduate is, in many cases, to be disenfranchised in social terms and disempowered in the job market. Moreover, the possession of a degree is a key credential not only to entry into the job market, but also to increasingly meritocratic forms of social status. Higher education is also a key element in the new, "post-Fordist" economy. Higher education is a major producer of the expert skills and knowledge on which such an economy depends at the high technology, high value-added end of the market. Higher education institutions are often a key element in rendering local and regional economies globally competitive, not only as suppliers of high quality expert skills and knowledge, but also by providing a research base that feeds directly into local economic development. However, as the massification of higher education proceeds, so possession of a degree ceases to be a "positional good," i.e. graduates as a group cease to be so socially distinctive. While exposure to higher education is increasingly a *sine qua non* of competitiveness in the labor market, it ceases to guarantee access to elite professional jobs. Hence, higher education must not only provide expert knowledge and high levels of attainment in difficult subjects, it must also emphasize the provision of generic and flexible skills.

These changes have coincided with fresh thinking about the role of government and even rethinking of public service values. By this I mean there has been a growing distrust of top-down planning and an increasing willingness instead to trust the efficacy of markets in allocating resources. Thus, as there has been a rethinking of the scale and purposes of the welfare state, higher education, as part of the public service, has not escaped the redefinition of government. Thus any consideration of the "governance" of the university sector raises issues about the relationship between the university sector and the state. If the state's business today is promoting economic competitiveness rather than social equity, what then does this say about the aims and purposes of higher education? And as the focus of state activity has shifted from planning inputs to auditing outcomes, is this a reinforcement of, or a demolition of, traditional notions of university autonomy?

The examples I use in this chapter will be drawn primarily from the U.K., although I certainly do not believe that the trends that I describe are unique to the U.K.; many of them can be observed across both Western Europe and North America.

GENERIC TRENDS IN MASS HIGHER EDUCATION

In 1994, the U.K. Committee of Vice-Chancellors and Principals established a long-term strategy group to provide a capacity for some long-term thinking on higher education policy. In September 1995, the group held a seminar on "Diversity in Higher Education," which included an enlightening paper by Martin Trow (1995). Trow identified a number of elements that constitute what he termed a "mature system of mass higher education." Trow listed 13 specific elements, but here I want to adapt his taxonomy and concentrate on five themes that I have somewhat arbitrarily grouped together as follows:

1. **Growth:** Trow argues that mature systems of mass higher education have at least 15 percent of the age grade entering higher education and in most advanced societies this can be rising to above 25 percent. The U.S. and Japan, for instance, are moving towards a system of "universal" higher education where over 50 percent of the age cohort now enter higher education. In the U.K., it has already been calculated that over 60 percent of the present population will, at some stage in their lifetime, experience higher education.

2. **Diversity:** This term can be interpreted in a variety of ways. On the whole, most commentators favor an increase in diversity in the higher education sector, but are divided over what it precisely means. There is also some confusion over whether diversity is best seen as a means—a variety of pathways towards a common degree standard—or an end—a variety of degree standards. In any case, the move towards a mass system of higher education has produced greater diversity of institutions in terms of their structure, organization, purpose, mission, etc. Inevitably, the growth of higher education also produces greater diversity among the student body, and indeed among the staff, with respect to their class

origins, ages, interests, and talents. This development, in turn, brings about an increasing diversity in curricula and pedagogy. Even when the new students are academically able, their interests and motivation will differ. As Trow comments, "People in the mass system can no longer assume that students will learn on their own; it comes to be doctrine that students can only be expected to learn what they are taught. That leads to a greater emphasis on teaching as a distinct skill that itself can be taught (and assessed), and places the student in the process of learning, rather than the subject, at the center of the educational enterprise, a Copernican revolution" (p. 2). Another cluster of changes implicit in the above also ensues: more modularization of courses, the emergence of credit transfer, and an increase in the numbers of mature, part-time, and working students. This development, in turn, points to the assimilation of continuing education with all its more mature vocationally oriented students into the system of higher education.

These trends are directly observable in the U.K. and have been compressed into a remarkably short space of time—less than a decade. As a result, they have produced considerable stresses in the British higher education system. For example, while the U.K. must continue to increase the number of people coming into higher education to provide the skills that will make the country competitive internationally, the nation cannot afford 104 leading research universities each striving to become like Oxford or Cambridge or Harvard or Heidelberg. Yet the nation needs *both* to ensure a continued supply of high quality people in an increasingly knowledge-based world *and* to maintain Great Britain's role at the leading edge of science, engineering, and technology. Because resources are grossly insufficient to achieve both of these objectives in all universities, we are witnessing the rapid differentiation of the university system in the U.K. Yet, the Dearing Committee was completely silent about the structural changes that might be necessary to cope with these stresses and strains.

3. **Quality and Standards:** The advent of a more diversified higher education system has led to a lengthy and agonized public debate on quality and standards. Trow argues that the growth and diversification of higher education, along with associated changes in pedagogy, require that society and its systems of higher education surrender any idea of broad common standards of academic performance between institutions and even between subjects within a single university. This surrender has been fiercely resisted in the U.K. where there has been a thriving, and sometimes acrimonious, debate over quality control and the enforcement of at least minimum threshold standards. The problem—although rarely articulated as such—is that if students gain their degrees with

widely varying levels of proficiency and attainment, then the meaning of the degree itself must change. The growth of diversity in the U.K. has led to a countervailing determination to narrow a band of permissible variability in levels of attainment. There has developed a massive "quality industry" to assure the output of the higher education system, but this in turn has been treated with deep suspicion by most of those in the academic profession (particularly in the older universities) who see quality control as a threat to academic autonomy. The shift from an elite to a mass system of higher education has therefore been accompanied by a shift from a connoisseurship approach to standards—"I know it when I see it"—to a more forensic approach—evidence-based quality control.

The introduction of this system of quality assurance control arises in part from the withdrawal of trust in professional self-regulation. In the mass higher education system, self-regulating connoisseurship soon becomes demystified as a legitimate form of quality control. As the system becomes larger and more diverse, quality has to become codified particularly because the system is now expensive and becoming more so, but also because individual national systems are increasingly benchmarked globally. While at one level this development can be seen as a straightforward trading standards issue with the degree as a commodity whose quality needs to be guaranteed, it also raises questions about autonomy, professional responsibility, and state control. While governments in the Western world have placed more faith in markets, they have placed less faith in professional self-regulation. Therefore, the present paradox in the U.K. is that the British university system is simultaneously underplanned and overregulated.

4. **Rise of Managerialism:** Perhaps a better way of phrasing this would be to borrow the title of A. H. Halsey's book, *The Decline of Donnish Dominion*. In a mass higher education system, traditional collegial self-governance becomes distinctly frayed around the edges. Institutional leadership tends to be characterized more in terms of the role of the chief executive rather than *primus inter pares*. To cope with the decline in real resources (see below), universities develop strengths and systems of line management while simultaneously cultivating a more entrepreneurial, expedient, and opportunistic frame of action as senior management strives to manage uncertainty and change. Senior management has become increasingly professionalized (albeit slowly and reluctantly in the U.K.), although the appropriate model for management in universities remains unclear.

5. **Declining Real Resources:** While governments may will the end of mass higher education, they rarely will the means. Growth in the system

is almost universally accompanied by declining real resources per capita student. This is because the economic forces driving the expansion of higher education are also those driving the desire to shrink the public sector. The end product is a kind of microcosm of the fiscal crisis of the state in respect of the provision of resources to the higher education sector. This outcome not only forces universities to cultivate alternative sources of financial support, especially in the private economy, but also produces a degree of convergence on private sector systems of management and organization—particularly those "post-Fordist" parts of the economy that lie in the service sector. However, many universities frequently experience a cultural lag. Most professional academics like to feel that their institution is "well managed"; nevertheless, "management" is still usually a pejorative term that makes some academics wince.

THE ROLE OF THE STATE

U.K. universities are, with one exception, in receipt of significant public funds. Yet they are, at the same time, legally independent private sector institutions. This inevitably creates tensions, but not necessarily conflict, between their requirement to account for the uses to which these public funds are put and their desire to retain their autonomy. The recent period of introspection in the U.K. has highlighted the danger of permitting funding to dominate a regime in which accountability is becoming contract or output oriented. The Dearing Committee was essentially set up to square the circle of increasing the size of the higher education system while decreasing its dependence upon the public purse. In many respects, the report has dealt with the symptoms rather than the cause. As a result, while universities are required to place emphasis on their response to market needs, the state (particularly in the form of its funding and monitoring agencies in the U.K.) continues to be highly intrusive.

One implication that might be drawn from this is that the government's interventionist approach in regulating quality control, value for money, etc. is a failure of trust in the self-governance of universities. It might also be regarded as an acknowledgment by government of the increasing importance of higher education in achieving economic competitiveness and social cohesion. Unfortunately, in the U.K., the recognition of this importance appears to go hand-in-hand with an increase in regulation.

What the Dearing Report has tried to achieve in the U.K. is a development of mechanisms that retain the fundamental autonomy of universities while rendering them simultaneously more accountable in their use of public funds. In many respects, the Dearing Report seeks to revive public and political trust in the British university system by explicitly advocating a compact between universities and their numerous stakeholders, whether employers, students, users of research, or government. Such a compact would contain a variety of elements, including the following:

- lifelong learning
- regional economic regeneration and development
- the creation of the learning society
- scholarship and pure research across and within disciplines
- technological innovation
- social cohesion
- public accountability

It remains to be seen how far this compact can hang together. But one suspects that this agenda is not so different in most advanced societies at the present time and that there is equally a widespread recognition that the higher education system is simply too important to be left to academics alone. How this view can be reconciled with traditional, liberal conceptions of university autonomy as a bulwark *against* the state also remains to be seen.

This balance can be described as a "managed market." Where education is financed mainly by public monies, the universities retain control of their own affairs while operating within centrally defined and regulated parameters managed by the funding agencies. Many of the main management problems within higher education stem from the tensions inherent in the notion of a managed market. In the name of accountability or quality assurance, intrusion into the hitherto "secret garden" of the university world has become extensive and onerous. The interface between the state and the university needs to be rethought, but nostalgia for a mythical golden age of university autonomy needs to be removed. In the U.K. at least, there has been a widespread belief that recent changes in the higher education system are merely a passing phase, after which there will be "a return to normal." There has also been a reluctance to recognize that the only thing that is normal is change itself.

In the U.K., therefore, attempts to redefine the relationship between the universities and the state have not been successful. As successive governments have sought to limit the rise in public spending, the only long-term policy with regard to higher education has been the enforcement of resource constraints, termed in Great Britain, with typically English hypocrisy, as "efficiency gains." The only real long-term policy has therefore been to limit the burden on the taxpayer of an expanding higher education system. This alone has been sufficient to produce major changes in the quality of the student learning experience and, to take another example, the ability of university teachers to meet their aspirations to undertake research. Such a policy has also produced a number of other consequences, whether intended or unintended.

1. There has been an increasing trend towards utilitarianism. The funding of higher education has been linked to short-term economic goals, i.e., higher education is seen as a means rather than an end in itself. As a result, higher education has come under increasing scrutiny from *external* stakeholders demanding a demonstration of value for money. The *users* of the higher education system (e.g., employers) have thus acquired an increased stake in determining higher education priorities. However, the higher education system itself has paid insufficient attention to how links with the various potential actual users can be organized in a manner that is as systematic, rigorous, and robust as that which has traditionally been developed among colleagues within the sphere of "donnish dominion." The academic world remains suspicious of full engagement with the users of its services, fearing that such contact will inevitably corrupt the integrity of the academic enterprise. This may have prevailed in an era when the universities held a monopoly position over the production of knowledge. However, it is simply not a realistic possibility now or in the foreseeable future.

2. Arguments set out for the allocation of resources to higher education in this new context now veer alarmingly between higher education as an investment and higher education as a cultural good. In the U.K., there is much public discussion about the cost of higher education and relatively little about the return. This in turn is linked to a shift in emphasis towards measuring in specific terms the quantifiable benefits of expanding higher education—the impact of performance indicators, management by objectives, etc. Peer review has declined as a legitimate method for allocating resources and is being increasingly replaced by a form of merit review that uses ulterior measures of quality.

Although, much of the paraphernalia and even the vocabulary of modern management is used increasingly in universities, the reality can be somewhat different. For example, the vocabulary of the marketplace is often used but the situation in the U.K. does not correspond in any way to any known market. The *vocabulary* of the market is used essentially to describe the pattern of student demand. In all other respects, there is simply no market in the higher education system. The state, through its associated agencies (e.g., the Funding Councils) sets student numbers, allocates student places, controls budgets, allocates resources, and devises penalties for over- or under-success (see Ryder, 1996, pp. 54-55). All this is done in the name of limiting public spending and obtaining value for money through quality control. The reality is a fundamental mistrust of the market. For example, if, as has recently been the case in the U.K., demand for places in science and engineering is falling, the funding agencies have ordained (until very recently) that the number of places should be sustained even if high quality students are hard to come by. On the other hand, in other subjects, such as law or medicine, where student demand is buoyant, the funding agencies have been reluctant to sanction a rapid expansion of places to meet revealed student demand. The end result bears an uncanny resemblance to central economic planning in 1950s Eastern Europe—all of this taking place using the vocabulary of market forces! This is not so much a managed market as the world of Gosplan, something which is neither a market nor properly planned. The Dearing Committee, while recognizing some of this, veered away from fully empowering students as consumers and allowing the market to clear. As Trow (1995) somewhat tartly observed, "the alternative ... is a heavier reliance on markets and competition, not yet in favor in most European countries" (p. 2).

NEW FORMS OF UNIVERSITY MANAGEMENT

It is often alleged that the trends referred to earlier in this chapter have produced an increasingly "top-down" style of management in universities. This may be true but it needs to be treated with a degree of caution. Anecdotes about the individual petty tyrannies of professors and heads of departments in universities are legendary and, if anything, many systems of university governance have become more open, transparent, and democratic today than in previous eras. Nevertheless, the sheer growth in size and complexity of the modern university has placed a greater reliance upon less face-to-face contact and more formal systems of management and control. Coffield (1995, p. 14) has, for example, argued that

> there has been a shift of power within universities *from* academics and *towards* administrators . . . . The need to respond quickly to a declining unit of resource and to the bureaucratic pressures created by the political insistence on "sharp accountability for results" (e.g. performance indicators in teaching and research, development plans etc.) have undercut one of the cherished traditions in British universities, namely collective self-government, and concentrated power in the hands of senior academic management.

This view is certainly widely held, but is perhaps somewhat exaggerated. As Coffield himself says elsewhere "collegiality is *not* appropriate for all decisions and academics are often wasting precious time on matters best dealt with by trained administrators" (p. 14). Academics have not, arguably, been particularly adept at surveying external trends, reexamining their assumptions and processes, and developing new practices and structures as a result.

This points to a lack of training for senior managers in higher education, particularly in the management of change. It also points to a lack of a widely accepted management model that can be effectively applied in higher educa-tion. Too often when the term "managerialism" is employed, it is a kind of caricature of Taylorism—a rigid top-down model of line management adapted from traditional forms of manufacturing industry. This kind of "command and control" management is not only inappropriate for universities, but is scarcely used any longer in many branches of manufacturing industry and certainly not in branches of other knowledge-based service sector organizations towards which universities are increasingly converging (e.g., the media, publishing, leisure services, etc.). Here the introduction of relatively flat management hierarchies (what does this say for the status of the professor?) and a devolved system of budgetary control can be viewed as attempts to provide a framework in which the talents of creative individuals can be fully expressed to ensure the competitiveness of the company concerned. This is not too far away from an appropriate management model for the university—one in which the manage-ment function becomes almost a service function rather than a command function, seeking to guarantee a framework in which highly talented individu-als can be motivated to realize their potential. What is lost here is not so much the sense of collegiality and self-governance as the erosion of traditional privilege. Donnish dominion was only ever enjoyed by a small proportion of the employees of a university. Has this really changed?

CONCLUSIONS

The governance of the university system is undoubtedly in a state of turbu-lence, the outcomes of which remain difficult to discern. From the point of view of many governments, the key task is to try to keep control of a system that actively *wants* to be out of control. However this implies that govern-ments know what they want and in the U.K., at least, this is a rather dubious assumption. The current situation is full of irony and paradox: overregulation and underplanning, the rhetoric of diversity and the reality of convergence on homogeneity, the commitment to expansion and the reduction of cost. One could go on. From the point of view of the academic community itself, there has been a marked inability to diagnose contemporary trends and to engage in real politics. The academic community has not exactly distinguished itself by marshalling arguments that could call upon widespread public support. The public at large remains alternately indifferent towards and hostile to the many privileges granted to higher education in comparison with other parts of the education sector. The academic community, too, has been ambivalent about the extent to which the growth of the higher education sector should be accompanied by an explicit hierarchical ordering of institutions. The term diversity has often been the euphemistic cloak to disguise this. Everyone in the U.K. is in favor of further diversity in higher education, but history tells us that the English, in particular, have a genius for converting diversity into hierarchy. As the system has expanded so has it differentiated; as it differentiates, it is more than likely that it will become more hierarchical. The situation already is tacitly accepted, but it is not explicit. Meanwhile, students and their parents are left to struggle to make sense of a tacitly hierarchical system that publicly speaks only in the vocabulary of diversity.

The Dearing Report was an opportunity to tackle some of these issues; but dominated by the sheer political necessity of finding a solution to the conundrum of the public funding of universities, it ducked many of the longer term, structural issues. To be fair, the committee seems to have recognized this itself. It contains the curious recommendation that a further inquiry be conducted in five years' time. In my view, this will be necessary. As the U.K. still seeks to come to terms with the rapid shift from an elite to a mass higher education system, many of the inherent tensions remain unresolved. Changes in structure, and not just in practice, are inevitable in my view. No activity takes place in the university that cannot, and does not, take place elsewhere. If the university sector does not itself come to terms with the new world in which it finds itself, the alternative may be the end of the university as we know it.

REFERENCES

Coffield, F. (1995). "Introduction and Overview" in Frank Coffield et al., eds., *Higher Education in a Learning Society*. Durham: University of Durham, School of Education.

Halsey, A.H. (1992). The *Decline of Donnish Dominion*. Oxford: Oxford University Press.

National Committee of Inquiry into Higher Education. (1997). *Higher Education in a Learning Society*. London: HMSO.

Ryder, A. (1996). "Reform and U.K. Higher Education in the Enterprise Era," *Higher Education Quarterly, 50 (1)*, pp. 54-70.

Scott, P. (1995). "Universities and the Wider Environment." Paper presented to the CVCP Seminar on Diversity in Higher Education, London, 14/15 September.

Trow, M. (1995). "Diversity in Higher Education in the United States of America." Paper presented to the CVCP Seminar on Diversity in Higher Education, London, 14/15 September.

CHAPTER 13

Information Age Challenges to Research Libraries

Crisis in the University of California Library System

Charles F. Kennel, with the collaboration of Sharon E. R. Franks

This contribution to the Glion Colloquium focuses on a crisis in the University of California (U.C.) library system. The predicament, faced by research institutions throughout Western industrialized countries, is the struggle to maintain access to scholarly publications in the face of concurrent growth in the quantity and cost of this material. In terms of its underlying causes, stakeholders, and potential solutions, the U.C. library crisis mirrors challenges facing higher education in general. A principal component of the problem is financial. Funding levels that have traditionally supported libraries are now insufficient to purchase and manage a growing volume of increasingly costly scholarly output. The present imbalance in funds and costs has deeper roots in an unsustainable system of scholarly publication, as well as broadening demands on university libraries in the Information Age, factors that are forcing a restructuring of the information marketplace. Players in this complex situation have diverse goals and expectations: faculty who expect access to journals in their fields of study regardless of cost, senior administrators and library directors responsible for library budgets, commercial publishers who dominate a monopoly-like marketplace in which prices have risen dramatically, and an increasingly diverse set of users. Finally, as with other issues confronting academic research institutions, addressing the library crisis requires involvement of all stakeholders and a search for creative solutions beyond campus boundaries.

Charles F. Kennel would like to thank Richard Lucier, the U.C. digital librarian, for his guidance in these matters.

SCOPE OF THE CRISIS

The crisis in the U.C. library system has manifested itself in reduction in acquisitions, staff cuts, and diminished diversity in collections at all nine U.C. campuses: Berkeley, San Francisco, Davis, Santa Cruz, Santa Barbara, Riverside, Los Angeles, Irvine, and San Diego. Managed by the Office of the President, the principal officers on each campus have forged beneficial collaborations among the nine research libraries, even though acquisitions have been historically handled independently. For the U.C. libraries, the fundamental survival issue has become how to rise to the new challenges of the Information Age in the face of diminishing resources for traditional functions.

Both the volume and price of scholarly work have increased nearly three-fold in the last decade (Association of Research Libraries et al. 1998), curtailing the libraries' ability to acquire new publications. Between 1992 and 1996, the price of materials purchased by U.C. libraries rose 30 percent while acquisition budgets increased only 10 percent. In the three-year period ending in 1996, acquisitions of monographs declined 13 percent (Kennel 1998). Drastic reductions have also been made in serial acquisitions, and this is not surprising considering that since 1986 median prices for scholarly journals increased at least 169 percent—more than three times the rate of inflation (Malakoff 1998). The rise in costs of scientific serials purchased by U.C. libraries has averaged 12 percent annually since 1992 (Kennel 1998). Costs of subscriptions to online databases grew even more rapidly—in one case 350 percent in a single year (Association of Research Libraries et al. 1998). Hesitant to fuel continued cost increases, but obliged to address faculty concern over acquisition reductions, U.C. chancellors have only reluctantly agreed to increase library acquisition budgets.

Along with shortfalls in collection budgets, U.C. libraries have also suffered staff reductions. U.C. Los Angeles, U.C. Davis, and U.C. Berkeley each lost 20 percent of their staff since 1991 (Kennel 1998). Pressure to acquire high-usage materials has also reduced the diversity of library collections. Campus acquisitions are becoming less comprehensive and more duplicative. Consequently, requests for interlibrary loans rose 50 percent since 1991, while requests for photocopies of material outside U.C. collections jumped 84 percent (Kennel 1998).

UNDERLYING ISSUES

A look into the causes of rising publication prices reveals an unstable system of scholarly communication. The commercialization of scholarly publication several decades ago has led to an arrangement where publishers control access to intellectual property produced by university faculty whose institutions, though they and their governments have subsidized the research on which these publications are based, are forced to pay for access to this information. In the case of digital information, publishers are now attempting to place restrictions on distribution and use that have not previously been applied to scholarly publications. While libraries have been the first partners in the scholarly communication system to feel the ill effects of this model, in the long term it will restrict the flow of scholarly discourse at all levels of university research and education.

At the same time they struggle to deal with the financial crunch imposed by increasing book and periodical costs, university libraries face the new and inescapable challenge of procuring and managing a burgeoning array of digital (electronic) information. They are also under new pressures to serve an expanding set of users, including distance and lifelong learners, in addition to traditional students and faculty. Developing strategies to meet the demands of the Information Age and serve an increasingly diverse student body are recurrent themes among leaders of institutions of higher education.

Within the U.C. system, libraries have struggled with increasingly severe financial difficulties for more than a decade, and they have exhausted their ability to deal with these problems using available resources. The library crisis has now become a university crisis. The U.C. Library Planning and Action Initiative Advisory Task Force concluded in its March 1998 *Final Report* that to solve the libraries' problems the university community would have to change, particularly in the area of scholarly communication (Kennel 1998). Libraries are becoming agents of change for universities in the Information Age.

PROPOSED SOLUTIONS

Acknowledging that the library crisis is multifaceted and ongoing, the University of California has formulated a set of strategic initiatives that include measures to strengthen resource sharing, acquire and distribute electronic materials, and even transform scholarly communication.

Resource Sharing

While the U.C. will continue to fund growth and maintenance of traditional print collections, economic constraints make it no longer practical for each campus library to build and maintain a comprehensive print collection. Striving for comprehensive *access* to scholarly publications, however, is a realistic goal. The U.C. Library Planning and Action Initiative Advisory Task Force has advocated an approach based on the philosophy of "one university, one library" (Kennel 1998). Collaboration among the nine U.C. campuses, as well as partnerships with other libraries, museums, and industry, will facilitate cost-effective access to diverse print and electronic materials. While the human and managerial problems of realizing these collaborations are challenging even for a relatively well-integrated multi-campus system like the U.C., resource sharing must leverage limited resources to build diverse collections at the systemwide level. This approach necessitates development and support of a system to facilitate expeditious access to printed materials from users' desktops. Overnight transport of print materials, collective purchasing of print materials and licensing of digital products, development of specialized local collections, and extensive digital networking within and beyond the U.C. system are key components of strengthening resource sharing.

The California Digital Library (CDL)

To provide leadership in support of a vision that integrates digital technologies into the creation of collections and improved access to information, the U.C. established the California Digital Library (CDL) in October 1997 as the "co-library" of the University of California. President Richard C. Atkinson made it a priority to secure a new appropriation from the State of California specifically for the CDL. A collaborative effort of all nine campuses, managed and coordinated by a small group at the Office of the President, the CDL acquires and manages electronic content in support of academic programs, supports digitization of paper-based materials, encourages new forms of scholarly communication, and assists campuses by providing user support and training.

As the key strategic initiative for meeting the challenges facing the U.C. libraries, the CDL is responsible for providing new services and extending existing ones to successfully transform the library system over the next decade. Successful polling of U.C. faculty resulted in digital collection priorities for the Science, Technology, and Industry Collection, the CDL's charter collection. This framework for making selection decisions for digital collections is being replicated for other disciplines. Negotiation of systemwide licenses at favorable discounts, innovative arrangements to share collections with other California-based institutions, and ongoing leadership in the effort to transform scholarly publishing are among the noteworthy accomplishments of the CDL. In the first year alone, the CDL has made access available to thousands of scholarly journals that would have cost the university more than $2 million in additional funds if the campuses had tried to provide the same level of access separately.

Transforming Scholarly Communication

University-wide support of a strong information infrastructure may encourage a much needed change in the current unsustainable model of scholarly communication. At the U.C., a Copyright Task Force has been appointed to examine redefinition of academic intellectual property rights. Proposed changes would protect intellectual property—both print and digital—from commercial exploitation to the detriment of the institution and its faculty. Transformation plans must provide for certification of scientific and scholarly work (e.g., peer review), as well as widespread dissemination of the results of research.

Reallocation of the $680 million spent annually by North American research libraries on acquisitions can exert a powerful influence on shaping the market for scholarly information (Association of Research Libraries et al. 1998). With such steps as expanded resource sharing and establishment of the CDL, the U.C. is attempting to regain a measure of control over the flow of scholarly information that sustains its research and teaching missions. Parallel courses undertaken by universities worldwide—possibly in partnerships with scholarly societies—could reshape the entire system of scholarly communication and potentially motivate changes in academic culture. In anticipation of times when forms of publication are more diverse than conventional books and journals, universities should encourage faculty leaders to begin thinking about broader criteria and more flexible processes for academic promotion.

Continuous Planning

In developing and articulating its multi-pronged approach to easing the library crisis, U.C. leaders anticipate that continuous innovation will be required over a decade-long transition from completely print-based holdings to integrated digital and paper collections. To be successful, plans must be created with contributions from all stakeholders in the university's library system—faculty, students, librarians, information technologists, and administrators. Library planning must be coordinated with the universities' technical and academic planning to address the needs of increasingly diverse and more numerous users. The cultural changes within the university are so great that no strategic plan for transformation is possible. Response to the library crisis will require continuous planning supported at the highest institutional levels. Conducted with vision and long-term commitment to innovation, the evolution of university libraries can serve as an instructive model for guiding the university in this complex transition and addressing other issues challenging institutions of higher education.

REFERENCES

Association of Research Libraries, Association of American Universities, Pew Higher Education Roundtable. (1998). "To Publish and Perish," *Policy Perspectives, 7 (4)*, pp. 1-11.

Kennel, C. F. (1998). *Final Report of the Library Planning and Action Initiative Advisory Task Force*. Berkeley: University of California.

Malakoff, D. (1998). "New Journals Launched to Fight Rising Prices," *Science, 282*, pp. 853-54.

CHAPTER 14

Lifelong Learning in the University

A New Imperative?

Alan Wagner

INTRODUCTION

To identify lifelong learning as a key, new orientation in the teaching mission of higher education is, in some respects, surprising. On the one hand, the first years of university studies already aim to provide a basis for further study and learning, as well as for taking on advanced level tasks in employment. At the same time, most policy statements on lifelong learning—from the European Commission's White Paper *Learning and Training: Towards the Learning Society* (European Commission 1995), the Delors Commission report entitled *Learning: The Treasure Within* (UNESCO 1996) and the report of the meeting of OECD education ministers entitled *Lifelong Learning for All* (OECD 1996) to a large number of policy statements and commission reports in a number of countries—embrace a wide range of learning, education, and training activities. Higher education is but one of the many activities and stages of learning coming under policy scrutiny. Indeed, the U.K. Green Paper on lifelong learning is marked by the limited attention it gives to higher education; the "University for Industry" that it includes is not a university at that term is commonly understood, nor is the initiative directed primarily at

This chapter draws on the background note prepared by Professor Suzy Halimi for the Glion Colloquium and some of the interventions at that meeting. However, the views expressed are the author's; they do not implicate the Organisation for Economic Cooperation and Development or the countries concerned.

higher education (Department for Education and Employment 1998). On the basis of this account, universities and tertiary education more generally have a small, if well-established and well-defined role in lifelong learning.

Yet, there are other indications of the need for a reinforced, if not re-formulated, role for universities in lifelong learning and some evidence of increased provision for it in higher education institutions and systems in many OECD countries. For example, in Great Britain, the U.K. National Committee of Inquiry into Higher Education, chaired by Sir Ron Dearing, issued its report under the title *Higher Education in a Learning Society* (National Committee of Inquiry into Higher Education 1997); in Australia, the report emerging from the review of higher education financing and policy, headed by Roderick West, carried the title *Learning for Life* (Commonwealth of Australia 1998). Those titles accurately convey the committees' views that the most promising and appropriate directions for higher education are best seen and situated in a broader lifelong perspective for learning and that there is great value in bringing new thinking from this perspective to the organization, content, methods, and timing of learning in higher education. The report of the OECD's most recent work examining developments and policies at a level of studies beyond secondary education, *Redefining Tertiary Education* (OECD 1998c), takes a similarly broad view, as signaled by use of the term "tertiary" rather than "higher" education.[1] Taken together, these observations suggest new expectations and perspectives for learning at this level and new demands, even if a broad lifelong learning approach does not yet figure prominently in system-level higher education policies and the programs, teaching, and learning of universities.

The purpose of this chapter is to explore and elaborate more fully the role tertiary education institutions, universities in particular, might be expected to play in lifelong learning and to explore possible implications for teaching. Lifelong learning, in this respect, can be seen both as a "mission" and as an "influence," the latter in the sense of the manifestation of new, or re-formulated, demands for learning at this level.

---

[1] Twelve OECD countries have thus far participated —Australia, Belgium (Flemish Community), Denmark, France, Germany, Japan, New Zealand, Norway, Portugal, Sweden, United Kingdom, and the United States (Commonwealth of Virginia)—leading not only to the comparative report *Redefining Tertiary Education* (OECD 1998c) but also "country notes" that are available through the home page of the Directorate for Education, Employment, Labour and Social Affairs at the OECD web-site [www.OECD.org.] The OECD defines "tertiary education" as a level or stage of studies beyond secondary education. Such studies are undertaken in tertiary education institutions, such as public and private universities, colleges, and polytechnics, and also in a wide range of other settings, such as secondary schools, work sites, and via free-standing information technology-based offerings and a host of public and private entities. "First years" is used in this paper to refer to studies that can lead to a first qualification recognized on the labor market. In these programs and studies, the volume and diversity of learners is greatest.

A LIFELONG LEARNING PERSPECTIVE IN HIGHER EDUCATION

As conceived by OECD education ministers, lifelong learning refers to a continuum of learning extending from the very early years to *troisième age*. In this respect, the concept goes wider than recurrent adult and nonformal education. It emphasizes learners, and learning in preference to sectors, segments, institutions, and boundaries—whether with respect to contents, methods, and contexts of teaching and learning. From this perspective, it is useful to draw out the main dimensions of a lifelong approach in higher education.

Current discussion tends to concentrate on a new expectation that graduates, after some time on the job, will return periodically as adults to the university for "updating" and "upgrading." This trend involves more than "second chance" opportunities for adults.[2] It is perhaps better expressed as "second bite" learning that is increasingly required to refresh and boost the stocks of skills and knowledge of earlier graduates, simply to keep pace with innovations in products and services of all types and the ways they are provided to those who demand and use them. Available data provide a mixed picture of the extent to which universities and other tertiary education institutions are meeting this demand. In its most recent examination of this topic, the OECD reported that, in the early 1990s, the university "share"of the volume of high-level professional education and training was 5-10 percent in Germany and 5 percent in France. In the United Kingdom, the United States, and Canada, the shares were higher, reaching nearly 30 percent in Canada (OECD 1995).

But a focus only on "second bite" learning would not cover fully the new or redefined aspects of lifelong learning in higher education. Participation of adults in regular degree or diploma programs constitutes another dimension of the "lifelong learning" demand. In many OECD countries, higher education is no longer solely the province of young adults. OECD indicators show that net enrollment rates have increased in the decade from the mid-1980s for 18- to 29-year-olds (the age band for which comparable data are generally available across the period). While the increase in enrollment rates is pronounced for those under age 25, significant increases also appear in the 26-29 age group (see Table 1).

---

[2] The distinction between upgrading and "second chance" motives is blurred. Some adults without higher education qualifications upgrade in their fields, and in so doing, receive such qualifications.

```
TABLE 1
```

TRENDS IN PARTICIPATION IN TERTIARY EDUCATION BY AGE, 1985-1996 [1,2]
(NET ENROLLMENT RATE, PUBLIC AND PRIVATE)

	Ages 18-21			Ages 22-25			Ages 26-29		
	1985	1990	1996	1985	1990	1996	1985	1990	1996
Belgium	24.5	-	39.6	7.2	-	15.4	1.5	-	4
Canada	25.5	28.9I	40.5	9.5	11.4I	21.9	3.0	3.4I	9.1
Denmark	7.4	7.4	8.5	16.3	17.9	23.5	8.2	9.3	12.1
Finland	9.3	13.6	18.2	17.3	20.7	28.8	7.9	10.2	13.6
France	19.4	24.6	36.0	10.0	11.8	18.6	4.3	3.9	4.4
Germany	8.8	8.5I	10.8	15.5	15.9I	17.2	8.9	10.4I	11.8
Ireland*	15.2	20.3	31.4	2.8	4.3	15.5	-	-	-
Netherlands	14.4	17.9	24.0	11.9	13.4	19.2	5.7	4.7	5.4
New Zealand	14.9	20.8	29.4	9.6	13.8	13.8	-	-	7.1
Norway	8.8	14.4	19.0	13.2	18.9	24.8	5.7	8.2	10.5
Portugal	5.8	-	19.3	5.4	-	16.0	2.3	-	6.1
Spain	14.9	21.2	27.3	10.6	13.5	19.8	4.0	4.5	6.2
Sweden	7.9	8.7	13.7	11.3	11.4	17.9	6.5	6.1	8.0
Switzerland	5.7	6.4	7.6	10.6	12.1	15.3	5.2	6.4	7.4
United Kingdom	-	16.1	26.9	-	4.7	9.4	-	-	4.8
United States	33.0	36.2	34.6	14.5	17.1	21.5	8.2	8.5	11.1
Average of above	14.4	16.8	24.2	11.0	12.8	18.7	5.5	6.5	8.1

-: missing value.
* Data for 22-25 age group include ages 26-29, and applies to 1995
1. Net enrollment rates based on head counts.
2. Vertical bars indicate a break in the series.

Sources: OECD (1997a) and OECD (1998a).

These patterns reflect increased rates of staying on and of returning, both to obtain additional qualifications and later entry.[3] With respect to the latter, there are distinct country patterns. While OECD data on new university entrants show, for example, that young adults in their late teens and early twenties predominate in France and Ireland, a somewhat older group of new entrants, in their early to late twenties, reflects the norm in Denmark and Sweden. Canada, Hungary, and New Zealand show a wide range of ages at first entry, from the late teens to mid-twenties (see Table 2). The data do not yet

---

[3] Rising rates of participation of older adults have other, less favorable explanations as well: Increased rates of queuing, failure, and associated delays to completion of studies at least partly arise from programs and teaching poorly geared to the needs and interests of students or to the demands from the labor market. This point is examined in greater detail below.

permit analyses of trends in age at first entry,[4] but it is clear in some countries that new policies implemented or under consideration introduce changes that could alter the age distribution of university students. New first university degrees, introduced as bachelor's degrees in Denmark and Portugal and discussed in France, for example, aim to allow students to leave the university with a qualification short of a long first degree. The new degree structures open up possibilities for learners to alter the timing of university entry, exit, and

TABLE 2			
AGE DISTRIBUTION OF FIRST-TIME UNIVERSITY ENTRANTS, 1996			
	20th percentile	Age at:* 50th percentile	80th percentile
Austria	20.1	20.4	23.4
Canada**	18.9	20.0	26.5
Czech Republic	21.4	23.6	29.4
Denmark	19.8	21.4	26.5
France**	18.3	18.9	20.0
Germany	20.1	21.6	25.0
Greece	18.5	19.4	20.5
Hungary	18.0	20.3	25.3
Ireland	18.0	18.6	19.4
Netherlands	18.7	20.2	24.0
New Zealand	18.4	19.2	25.6
Norway	20.2	22.7	>29
Poland	19.5	20.6	23.2
Sweden	20.2	21.3	23.4
Switzerland**	20.1	21.2	23.2
Turkey**	18.4	19.9	23.1
United Kingdom	18.5	19.5	24.3
United States	18.3	19.0	24.2

* 20/50/80 percent of new entrants are below this age
** 1995

Source: OECD (1998a) and earlier volumes.

[4] Research in some countries reveals that those who delay entry into university studies are less likely to succeed. The interpretation and explanations for these results are several, but it seems likely that further adaptations in teaching to take into account the particular circumstances and motivations of these students could improve success rates and progress to degree completion. For the findings, see, e.g., U.S Department of Education (1997) and OECD (1997b).

return. On the other hand, in New Zealand, where there is a long tradition of adult participation in tertiary education, a "study right" policy provides universities and other tertiary-level providers with larger tuition subsidies for students who are enrolling for the first time and are *under* 22 years old (the "study right" applies for three years). The policy aims to encourage institutions to enroll young students.[5]

Further, a lifelong learning perspective redefines an orientation for study programs in the first years of tertiary education, extending back to lower levels of education and forward to adult needs and learning. As participation rates for young adults continue to rise throughout the OECD area, the principal transition to work for an increasing proportion of the age group takes place after tertiary, not secondary, education. If there is a public interest in enabling everyone to acquire the skills and abilities needed in a dynamic economy, this interest increasingly will be met through even higher rates of participation in tertiary-level studies. In the first instance, universities and other tertiary education institutions will be expected to assume a greater responsibility for those who may (or should) now aspire to studies at this level but have, until the present, not entered programs. This responsibility will extend to encouraging and enabling all who enter tertiary education to learn and succeed; the costs of failure in higher education for the individual, the economy, and society are now too great. The responsibility extends even further, to preparing individuals to undertake continuous learning and re-learning in a graduate labor market likely characterized by more frequent and varied job and career changes. Notwithstanding the need for universities to widen learning options for returning graduates, first-degree study programs will need to help students develop the capacity to adapt and to learn in new areas and new ways.

Taken together, these developments and policy interests suggest that a lifelong learning perspective in university and other tertiary education programs now takes on several dimensions:

- **foundation learning** for all students of any age, a long-standing aim to prepare higher education students for further study as well as entry into working life—but now conceived more broadly to encompass the need to better prepare graduates to undertake re-learning as they experience over their lifetime more frequent and more substantial changes among career tracks and fields

---

[5] The policy has been reconsidered because it has had the unintended effect of generating lower levels of public funding to institutions serving target populations.

- **expanded options** for young secondary school graduates who now require advanced-level skills, knowledge, and dispositions to be able to take advantage of emerging employment opportunities and be prepared to meet demands in the economy and society
- **second chance** for older adults who missed the opportunity when they were younger
- **second bite** for graduates, now seen as the most rapidly growing need and, as indicated, a possible consequence of new policies under discussion or implemented in several countries

Not all these dimensions are new to universities, but underlying changes in the economy and society, as well as in the profiles of learners, combine to recast the more conventional dimensions and to greatly increase the number of students who come under the less conventional ones. In most countries, demand—individual and social—is giving weight and re-definition to all these dimensions; all of them will need to be dealt with in programs, teaching, and learning. And, perhaps most significantly, differences in profiles and motivations of learners in individual programs and learning options are now as likely to be driven by demand as by the design and aims of the programs and options. Thus, for example, large proportions of full-time students, are working part- or full-time; graduates, first-time students and adults with no specific degree aims may be found in the same study program; and open learning or nondegree courses are no longer followed only by those without degree aspirations. The reality is that all teaching will need to take into account diversity in interests and aims and a reinforced and reformulated demand for lifelong learning.

The value of applying this more complex, broadly based and widely applicable view of lifelong learning to the teaching mission in the university is to stimulate new thinking and reflection and to change the terms of discussion with a view to help ministries, as well as institutions, develop and refine policies for programs, teaching, and learning. Some of the implications are identified and developed in the next section.

IMPLICATIONS FOR TERTIARY-LEVEL PROGRAMS, TEACHING AND LEARNING

Among others, the following four areas can be identified for attention and development in response to a new lifelong learning imperative in higher education:

- accommodating diverse patterns in the timing of studies
- introducing new pedagogical approaches, tools, and conditions
- transforming curricula
- focusing on learning and success

An implication for higher education of diverse patterns in the timing of entry, exit, and return—a pattern of lifelong learning—is that the relationship between the learner and the university continues later into adult life. Current students can be expected to return, in increasing numbers, to complete degree programs or to undertake further studies. On the basis of analysis of results of the International Adult Literacy Survey (IALS), undertaken by several OECD countries, that flow of returners could present a wider range of skills than might otherwise be assumed. For the IALS survey, "literacy skills" are defined as the ability to understand and employ printed information in daily activities and to use such information to achieve one's goals and to develop one's knowledge and potential.[6] Performance on the tests has been grouped into five literacy skill levels, Level 1 being the lowest and Level 5 the highest. According to those who have prepared the tests, Level 3 is regarded as a minimum level of competence needed to cope with the complex demands of everyday work and life. For 16- to 65-year-olds who have completed tertiary education, the proportions who fall below this threshold (on the prose scale) are above 10 percent in the seven countries examined, and, in some countries, the proportions exceed 30 percent (see Table 3).

The reasons for these proportions and inter-country differences are many, and the IALS tests provide only one set of measures of what adults know and are able to do. Whatever the explanations and measures, the findings lead to an important set of questions for universities and other tertiary education institutions as they assume even greater responsibility for lifelong learning: How can programs and teaching minimize the numbers of graduates who lack these skills and other requisite knowledge and dispositions? How can all programs and teaching—from regular degree studies to more specific modules—be adapted to take into account (indeed, boost) the varied levels of skills, knowledge, and dispositions represented in the pool of learners returning to higher and tertiary education as older adults?

---

[6] Literacy proficiency was assessed in three domains: prose, document, and quantitative. Details on definition and methodology are contained in the reports emerging from this work, among which are OECD and Statistics Canada (1996, 1997) and Murray, Kirsch, and Jenkins (1997).

TABLE 3

PERCENTAGE OF ADULTS WITH TERTIARY EDUCATION AT EACH LITERACY LEVEL (PROSE SCALE), 1994*

	% with level of education	Level of performance on IALS prose scale		
		Level 1/2	Level 3	Level 4/5
		(percentage)		
Canada				
University	16	11.0	29.8	59.1
Other tertiary	17	25.3	46.9	27.7
Germany				
University	12	21.0	39.4	39.6
Other tertiary	4	18.1	49.2	32.6
Netherlands				
University	18	13.2	52.3	34.5
Other tertiary	a	a	a	a
Poland				
University	7	41.6	42.0	16.4
Other tertiary	7	50.6	40.7	8.6
Sweden				
University	12	7.0	32.2	60.7
Other tertiary	13	10.8	43.4	45.8
Switzerland (French)				
University	14.	18.2	49.4	32.4
Other tertiary	9	32.6	56.8	10.7
Switzerland (German)				
University	7	27.8	46.7	25.5
Other tertiary	11	36.9	54.1	9.0
United States				
University	22	16.8	35.7	47.5
Other tertiary	15	34.3	39.9	25.8

*The data are based on tests administered in each country to samples of 2,500 to 3,000 adults broadly representative of the civilian, noninstitutionalized population aged 16-65. Individuals provided background information and described learning activities in an interview of about 20 minutes; literacy was assessed on the basis of responses to a set of tasks of varying degrees of difficulty. The test booklet was designed for completion in about 45 minutes. The section covering prose literacy was intended to assess the level of knowledge and skills to understand and use information from texts, including editorials, news stories, poems, and fiction. Details on methodology and scaling are provided in the publications from the survey.

Source: OECD and Statistics Canada (1996).

New pedagogical approaches are also needed, both to respond to diversity in the backgrounds, learning styles, and interests of students, young as well as older adult, and to promote and sustain the skills and dispositions needed by all to be lifelong learners. In one of the few comprehensive studies of how first degree courses do or do not prepare students as lifelong learners, Philip Candy and his colleagues identify a number of promising and effective teaching strategies (Candy, Crebert, and O'Leary 1994):

1. peer-assisted and self-directed learning
2. experiential and real-world learning
3. resource-based and problem-based teaching
4. development of reflective practice and critical self-awareness
5. as appropriate, open learning and alternative delivery mechanisms

These approaches are not new to universities: Peer tutoring has been introduced into the first year of university studies in France, and work-based learning may be found in some programs and institutions in France, the U.K., and the U.S. Significant numbers of part-time students are found both in countries where such a status is officially recorded and in countries where full-time students actually undertake less than a full courseload (see Table 4). Distance learning, sometimes drawing on information and communications technology (ICT), has developed in many forms in Australia, New Zealand, Japan, the U.S., the U.K., and Germany, among other countries.

Notwithstanding effective and promising initiatives, the experience across OECD countries is uneven, if not limited (Teichler 1998). While students and adult learners in many countries are expected to follow courses with minimum supervision, methods in study programs and other learning modules tend not to feature resource-based or problem-based teaching or to encourage and support self-directed learning, reflection, and critical thinking. Further, the potential of ICT to help foster learning and to respond to new lifelong learning demands has thus far been weakly and unevenly realized, owing to too little investment in instructional design and staff development. Generally, teaching practices and orientations remain poorly suited for addressing the needs and learning styles of the "new" lifelong learners in universities and other tertiary education institutions; insufficient to develop in the more "traditional" student a broader orientation toward lifelong learning; and to some extent insensitive to the reality of the diverse profiles of students (even so-called "traditional" students) now found in classrooms, laboratories, or distance learning course modules.[7] As universities and other tertiary education institu-

---

[7] For example, in Denmark, "regular" students may sometimes attend comparable open education courses in the institutions in which they enroll. In France, new policy initiatives promoting lifelong learning in higher education call for a new type of award for which credit could be given in regular degree programs.

tions increasingly cater in the same study program or learning option to a mix of students with different profiles and different interests, the challenge will be to make use of a combination of methods in every program or option.

To realize these kinds of changes, policy targets might be identified in several areas. A key target is staff policy, including new recruitment criteria (as has been discussed with regard to pedagogical preparation for university and other tertiary education staff in Germany) and the evaluation of and profes-

TABLE 4

DISTRIBUTION OF STUDENTS BY MODE OF ENROLLMENT AND SEGMENT, 1996

	University		Other Tertiary	
	Full-time	Part-time	Full-time	Part-time
Australia	60.1	39.9	20.2	79.8
Austria	100.0	a	90.6	9.4
Belgium	99.1	9.9	81.8	18.2
Canada	69.0	31.0	62.0	38.0
Czech Republic	91.8	8.2	100.0	n
Denmark	100.0	a	100.0	a
Finland	100.0	n	100.0	n
Germany	100.0	a	83.1	16.9
Greece	100.0	a	100.0	n
Hungary	68.3	31.7	a	a
Ireland	89.7	10.3	66.2	33.8
Italy	100.0	a	100.0	a
Japan	91.5	8.5	96.4	3.6
Korea	100.0	n	100.0	n
Luxembourg	100.0	n	m	m
Mexico	100.0	a	100.0	a
Netherlands	a	a	80.9	19.1
New Zealand	66.0	34.0	47.6	52.4
Norway	82.3	17.7	72.5	27.5
Spain	m	m	100.0	n
Sweden	72.7	27.3	x	x
Switzerland	100.0	a	45.7	54.3
United Kingdom	73.5	26.5	39.0	61.0
United States	70.4	29.6	36.0	64.0
Country mean	87.6	12.4	73.4	21.8

a category does not apply
m data not available
n magnitude is negligible or zero
x data included in other category or column

Source: OECD (1998a).

sional development for teaching, particularly in the extent and effectiveness of use of different methods and teaching support (as for example, in the Flemish Community of Flanders, where some staff resources are set aside at universities specifically to provide support for students who can benefit from augmenting conventional teaching with different methods available in student learning centers). Incentives can be more closely tied to the development and effective use of new teaching skills and approaches. New conditions for teaching and learning represent yet another important policy target in support of new pedagogical approaches, and here a lifelong learning orientation may favor new choices. For example, a major university in Australia considered the choice between building or re-equipping conventional classroom and lecture centers or finding a new balance through information technology-based instruction to support learning in different ways and at different places than in the past. Another option, encountered in two universities—one in the United Kingdom and one in the United States—is a purpose-built facility that brings together under one roof library, computing, and student services and academic support and student activities, as well as social activities and services commonly found in student centers. In these two institutions, the facilities operate from early morning until well into the night. In the U.K. university, the facility figures prominently in the organization of teaching and learning—first-year students follow course modules that introduce them to resources and support on site and aim to equip them for "learning in a constrained environment." While that phrase referred to constraints on university resources, the approach adopted implicitly responds to constraints on student time. As expressed in one country participating in the OECD work, "students are busy, too." That statement was made in reference to younger adults, but it applies with equal if not more weight to "new" lifelong learners in higher education. In all these areas, such initiatives as exist need to be broadly conceived to embrace the motivations, learning styles, and backgrounds of a wider profile of learners, and to be extended widely in specific modules organized for recurrent learning, as well as in regular study programs.

A third area for development and policy attention is to transform curricula to embody in graduates the capacities to be lifelong learners. This is not only, or even primarily, a matter to be dealt with in only certain types of programs or institutions. As already suggested, all students, whether in university first degree programs or other tertiary education short-cycle vocationally oriented programs, will need to be lifelong learners in the broadest sense. On several accounts, current programs and practices do not enable and encourage students to become lifelong learners (Candy, Crebert, and O'Leary 1994). Candy and his colleagues conclude that

courses which enhance lifelong learning: (1) provide a systematic introduction to
the field of study; (2) offer a comparative or contextual framework for the
viewing of the field; (3) seek to broaden the student and provide generic skills;
(4) offer some freedom of choice and flexibility in structure; and (5) provide for
the incremental development of self-directed learning. (p. xii)

This listing conveys a sense of the new orientations needed. An emphasis is on
organizing and conceiving study programs in such a way as to prepare graduates
to take on responsibility for their own learning. The need to do so is evident.
According to a recent survey of learning undertaken in Canada, those in the
labor force (or expecting soon to enter it) already spend about six hours per
week in employment-related *informal* learning, or about double the average
time they spend in formal education (Livingstone 1998). Such informal learning activity will likely increase, and steps should be taken to prepare individuals to make the most effective and efficient use of the considerable time and
other resources invested in it.

The realization of these changes in content and organization would require,
in the first instance, an opening up of first university degree courses now
conceived only in relation to specific professions or career tracks, and a rethinking of the contents and methods of those courses now conceived in this
way but already used as "general education" for a wider range of employment
destinations and as a "foundation" for later changes in career tracks. The
initiative undertaken by the French, German, Italian, and U.K. ministers to
"harmonize" a first, short qualification (the Sorbonne Agreement) provides
an opportunity for reflection, redefinition, and reorganization of studies, as
does the introduction of new bachelor's degrees in Danish and Portuguese
universities. In Japan, the United States, and the United Kingdom, where the
first university degree has a more general orientation, initiatives to strengthen
teaching and learning have involved closer attention to clarity in learning
aims, emphasis on cross-curricular learning and skills, and improved coherence and better integration between general and specialized elements in study
programs. These opportunities and initiatives offer scope to modify the contents and organization of learning in the first university degree to better
prepare graduates to be lifelong learners. At the same time, they can lead to a
different content and organization for studies that come after this first qualification: more focused, spanning disciplinary boundaries and exploiting knowledge bases within and outside of the university.

Finally, the new lifelong learning imperative emphasizes learning, not
teaching. In this perspective, the measure of quality is the extent to which
younger and older adults actually learn. For students following first degree
programs, failure is not acceptable; it is costly and demotivating at a time when
the need is to develop in everyone a capacity and desire for learning and re-

learning over a lifetime. The scale of the problem is evident. Survival rates, for example, vary from 90 to 35 percent across a selected set of OECD countries. Survival rates do not appear to be associated with overall participation rates (drop-out seems relatively low in the United Kingdom and Japan, for example, where participation rates are above the OECD average, and relatively high in Austria, where overall participation rates are below average). There appears to be a slight association between drop-out rates and the length of program, in that those countries with long first university degrees show somewhat lower survival rates than countries with short first university degrees (see Table 5). The pattern, however, is not uniform and does not provide a view of changes in drop-out rates over time. On this last point, in Germany and Belgium (French Community), among other countries, rates of drop-out increased over the 15- to 20-year period to the early 1990s. In both systems named, this period was marked by growth in participation in tertiary education (Moortgat 1996).

At present, too little is known about the nature of the drop-out and failure problem. In some cases, the numbers themselves are misleading; perhaps a quarter of those who drop out in Italy may be students who were registered but neither attended classes nor sat examinations. Further, failure in the first year is not the same as drop out, and some who drop out of one program may do so to complete studies in another program (see Table 6). In both cases, it is possible to refer to an eventual successful outcome, even if questions can be raised about effectiveness, efficiency, and costs of provision and organization of studies. In some cases, learners may not seek a qualification; they may leave to take up employment before completing degree requirements and perhaps wish to return at a later stage. The numbers are sufficiently large to suggest more serious difficulties with programs of teaching and learning for a much more diverse population of students. In a number of countries, an emerging policy position is that the "university experience" is not enough; a high failure rate increasingly will be seen as an indicator of programs and teaching poorly adapted to diverse learning needs and interests rather than an indicator of quality and quality control. Paradoxically, the former is often seen as the relevant criterion for quality (learning outcomes) in more specific, sometimes nondegree learning options offered to adults. This is less often the case in regular first degree study programs.

TABLE 5

RATES OF SURVIVAL AND DROP OUT IN UNIVERSITY-BASED EDUCATION

	Year of Reference	Year of Entry Complete	No. of Years to	Method	Source	Survival Rate	Drop-out Rate
Australia	1996	1994	3	Cross-section cohort	OECD database	65	35
Austria	1996	1989	7	Cross-section cohort	National calculation	53	47
Belgium (Flemish Community)	1996	~	~	Cross-section cohort	OECD database	63	37
Czech Republic	1995	1992	4	Cross-section cohort	OECD database	79	21
Denmark	1995	~	~	Synthetic cohort	National calculation	67	33
Finland	1996	1985	5	True cohort	National calculation	75	25
France	1995	1991	5	Cross-section cohort	OECD database	55	45
Germany	1995	1990	6	Cross-section cohort	OECD database	72	28
Hungary	1996	~	~	Synthetic cohort	National calculation	81	9
Ireland	1995	1992	4	Cross-section cohort	OECD database	77	23
Italy	1996	1991	6	Cross-section cohort	OECD database	35	66
Japan	1995	1992	4	Cross-section cohort	OECD database	90	11
Mexico	1996	1992	5	Cross-section cohort	National calculation	68	32
Netherlands	~	~	~	True cohort	National calculation	70	30
New Zealand	1995	1992	4	Cross-section cohort	OECD database	76	24
Portugal	1993	1991	3	Cross-section cohort	OECD database	49	51
Switzerland	1996	1991	6	Cross-section cohort	OECD database	74	30
Turkey	1995	1992	4	Cross-section cohort	OECD database	55	45
United Kingdom	1996	~	~	Weighted cross-section	National calculation	81	19
United States	1994	1990	4	True cohort	National calculation	63	37

Source: OECD (1998a).

TABLE 6

NONCOMPLETION RATES IN TERTIARY EDUCATION IN SELECTED OECD COUNTRIES[1]
(VARIOUS YEARS, PERCENTAGES)

	Fail in first year	Fail to complete program	Fail to complete any program
Belgium (Flemish Community), 1994			
University	47	34	
Non-university (one-cycle)	50	39	
Belgium (French Community), 1992-94			
University	56–62	57	
Non-university	60	38	
Denmark, 1995			
Tertiary		40	23
France, 1993[2]			
Total tertiary, excl. Sections de Techniciens Supérieurs		27	
University Institutes of Technology		20	
Italy, late 1980s			
Tertiary			64
Germany, 1993-94			
Tertiary			29–31
United Kingdom, 1995			
Tertiary			6–13

1. Figures have been drawn from several sources, and are therefore subject to differences in coverage and methodology. For definitions and methodology, readers are referred to the sources mentioned.
2. The figures refer to those who changed programs or dropped out after the first year; first-cycle only.

Sources: Belgium (French Community), Germany, Italy, United Kingdom: Moortgat (1996); Belgium (Flemish Community): Verhoeven and Beuselinck (1996); Denmark: Ministry of Education (1997); France: Ministère de l'Éducation nationale, de l'Enseignement supérieur et de la Recherche, Les entrants et les accédants (1993) (tabled data supplied for OECD "Thematic Review of the First Years of Tertiary Education"). See also OECD (1997a).

An emphasis on learning and success also opens up the university to play a more active role in bridging the gap between secondary education and tertiary-level studies and, indeed, among all providers and levels of education. Its most immediate implication is for the university to assume a shared responsibility with secondary education for the student through, for example, greater cross-level sharing of teaching and deeper, more varied contexts and methods for teaching and learning at the tertiary level. As noted by Wagner (1998), such a direction is challenging but not new. Counseling and information initiatives in secondary schools and support for student-centered teaching and learning in universities has figured in recent initiatives in France and Belgium (Flemish Community). In some U.S. institutions, the distinction between "remedial" and introductory "general" education may be blurring. What is in question here is not whether students are well-prepared for study in the university. Regardless of their preparations, the interests and learning styles in the larger pool of students are more varied than in the past, and the proportion of the adult population seeking and participating in study and learning options of all types based in universities and other tertiary education institutions will likely increase over time.

CONCLUSION

A lifelong approach to learning emphasizes the acquisition, use, and re-learning of knowledge and skills throughout adult life. Given already near-universal completion of a full cycle of secondary education, as well as rising rates of participation in studies of all types beyond the secondary level, much of what young and older adults now seek is flexible learning options at the tertiary level—to commence, combine, upgrade, or augment their knowledge and skills. Yet, access to and success in available learning opportunities are uneven, and the range of options and their quality are limited. There are both gaps with respect to the target groups reached and, in some countries, relatively weak representation of older adults when viewed against a lifelong approach to learning. Information technologies, distance and dual-mode institutions, and new partnerships among providers and between educational institutions and employers and community-based initiatives represent key growth points. They require a new approach to the policy infrastructure for education. The infrastructure must support learning occurring in a variety of ways, at different times and in different places as well as new orientations reflected in programs, teaching, and learning in universities and other tertiary education institutions.

The argument in this chapter is that a new need for continuous learning over a lifetime is giving rise to demands from individuals, employers, and public interests to reshape the contents, organization, and methods of programs and teaching in universities and other tertiary education institutions. The demands go beyond conventional recurrent education for the highly qualified to encompass new opportunities for new learners and a new orientation in conventional first degree programs to prepare graduates to be lifelong learners in the broadest sense.

The demands will be met in different ways by different types of institutions and programs, and different approaches may be found and introduced in individual programs within the same institution. A pro-active approach for the university, as advanced in general terms by one participant in the Glion Colloquium, is to aim for a relatively smaller share of enrollment, education, and lifelong learning but to find ways to build up linkages of its efforts in each of these areas. Such an approach could lead to an even more substantial contribution to meeting the new lifelong learning imperative in higher and tertiary education.

Whatever approach is adopted, every university will need to take into account wider developments in tertiary-level education and learning—indeed, in lifelong learning—not least to recognize the diversity in the profiles of qualifications, learning experiences, and interests of their own potential students and possible new links and interfaces with other education providers at the secondary, tertiary, and adult levels. One implication of the present context and policy drive favoring a lifelong learning approach is that it introduces an orientation and direction in which, as Alexander (1998) points out, the *complementarity of interests* in teaching and learning can be developed and supported. In this respect, no sector or set of institutions can set itself apart; policies will continue to promote solutions on a broader and cooperative basis.

REFERENCES

Alexander, T.J. (1998). *From Higher to Tertiary Education: Directions for Change in OECD Countries*. Statement for UNESCO World Conference on Higher Education, Paris, October 6.

Candy, P.C., Crebert G., and O'Leary, J. (1994). *Developing Lifelong Learners through Undergraduate Education*, Commissioned Report No. 28, National Board of Employment, Education and Training, Canberra, Australia.

Commonwealth of Australia. (1998). "*Learning for Life.*" *Review of Higher Education Financing and Policy* (West Review), Final Report, Canberra, Australia.

Department for Education and Employment. (1998). *The Learning Age: A Renaissance for a New Britain*. London: The Stationery Office.

European Commission. (1995). *Teaching and Learning: Towards the Learning Society*. Luxembourg: Office for Official Publications of the European Union.

France. (1993), *Ministère de l'Éducation national, de l'Enseignement supérieur et de la Recherche, Les entrants et les accédants: peincipales caractéristiques—Pouruites dans la filière et réorientations après 7 ans des entrants de 1993.*

Livingstone, D. (1998). *The Education-Jobs Gap*. Toronto: Garamond Press.

Ministry of Education (1997). *Communication to the Secretariat*. Danish Ministry of Education.

Moortgat, J.L. (1996). *A Study of Dropout in European Higher Education*. Strasbourg: Council of Europe.

Murray, T.S., Kirsch, I.S., and Jenkins L., eds. (1997). *Adult Literacy in OECD Countries: Technical Report on the International Adult Literacy Survey*. Washington, DC: National Center for Education Statistics, U.S. Department of Education.

National Committee of Inquiry into Higher Education. (1997). *Higher Education and the Learning Society*. London: HMSO.

OECD. (1995). *Continuing Professional Education of Highly-Qualified Personnel*. Paris: OECD.

———. (1996). *Lifelong Learning for All*. Paris: OECD.

———. (1997a). *Education Policy Analysis 1997*. Paris: OECD.

————. (1997b). *Thematic Review of the First Years of Tertiary Education, Country Note: Commonwealth of Virginia.* Paris: OECD.

————. (1998a). *Education at a Glance: OECD Indicators 1998.* Paris: OECD.

————. (1998b). *Education Policy Analysis 1998.* Paris: OECD.

————. (1998c). *Redefining Tertiary Education.* Paris: OECD.

OECD and Statistics Canada. (1996). *Literacy, Economy and Society.* Paris and Ottawa: OECD and Statistics Canada.

————. (1997). *Literacy Skills for the Knowledge Society: Further Results from the International Adult Literacy Survey.* Paris and Ottawa: OECD and Statistics Canada.

Teichler, U. (1998). "Lifelong Learning as a Challenge for Higher Education: The State of Knowledge and Future Research Tasks." Keynote presentation for Fourteenth General Conference of IMHE Member Institutions, Paris, September 7-9.

UNESCO. (1996). *Learning: The Treasure Within* (The Delors Report). Paris: UNESCO.

U.S. Department of Education. (1997) *The Condition of Education 1997.* Washington, DC: U.S. Government Printing Office.

Verhoeven, J.C. and Beuselinck, I. (1996). *Higher Education in Flanders (Belgium): A Report for the OECD, Ministry of the Flemish Community.* Paris: OECD.

Wagner, A. (1998). *Tertiary Education and Lifelong Learning: Perspectives, Findings and Issues from OECD Work.* Higher Education Management.

PART 4

• • • • • • • • • • • •

The University of the Future

CHAPTER 15

Higher Education in the Twenty-first Century

A European View

Jacob Nüesch

THE SOCIETAL ENVIRONMENT

We are presently living in the midst of the kind of transformation described by Peter F. Drucker in his book *Post-Capitalist Society* (1993): "Within a few short decades, society rearranges itself—its world view; its basic values; its social and political structure; its arts; its key institutions." We all believe that on our way into the twenty-first century we are developing a post-capitalist society—often defined as the "knowledge society"—that will be characterized and shaped by two major elements—life sciences and communication technologies. This transformation process has obviously been going on since the end of the Second World War, but the collapse of the communist system was a most profound milestone in our recent development. The onset of a far-reaching globalization and trade liberalization process has not made the world more harmonious. Although some believe the world will become better, others fear the dominance of an inhuman neoliberalism as taught by the Chicago School of Economics. The world is indeed in a transitory state with all the inherent risks and chances.

The current world situation is characterized by the following discrepancies and asymmetries:

- demographic growth in the southern hemisphere and economic growth in the northern hemisphere

- great disparities in wealth and quality of life between the northern and southern hemispheres
- exponential growth of knowledge and know-how, in particular in the northern hemisphere
- separation between financial flows and trade in manufacturing and services
- shift in power from the strictly vertical hierarchical state organizations to non-governmental organization-like networks without a center but with multiple nodes where groups of individuals or collectives interact for different purposes
- scarcity of work opportunities due to new and continuously changing technologies
- a continuous race for ever-increasing quantitative growth
- incongruity between the hope of the poor to consume and devour resources at the same pace as the rich societies and the limited global potential of our planet
- no society on earth yet lives in a sustainable way
- human society is plagued by a multitude of increasingly intra-national or regional conflicts
- human rights and, even more, humanitarian rights are less and less respected

However, despite these problems, the potential to adapt and to improve is huge; as Paul M. Kennedy wrote in his book *Preparing for the Twenty-First Century* (1994): "Global society is in a race between education and catastrophe."

THE ROLE OF RESEARCH AND HIGHER EDUCATION IN THE NEXT CENTURY

Today, basic research and higher education are more and more brought into question. This questioning cannot be explained by financial reasons alone; there are additional factors arising from the rapidly changing globalized world. The two following statements by influential Americans illustrate this situation most impressively:

> Progress in the war against disease depends upon a flow of new scientific knowledge. New products, new industries, and more jobs require continuous additions to knowledge of the laws of nature, and the application of that knowledge to practical purposes. Similarly our defense against aggression demands new knowledge, so that we can develop new and sophisticated weapons. This essential new knowledge

can be obtained only through basic scientific research. (Vannevar Bush 1945)

Yet advances in science and technology have not translated into leadership in rates of literacy or equality of opportunity. Neither have they overcome failing education systems, decaying cities, environmental degradation, unaffordable health care, and the largest national debt in history. (George Brown, chairman of the U.S. Science, Space, and Technology Committee, 1992)

In our economy-driven time, the return on investment in science and higher education in its current form is indeed questioned. Particularly in Europe, the demand for a more utilitarian approach is widely heard. It is also true that universities on their side were reluctant to get into close contact with industry, since they believe that by doing so their basic mission to create fundamental knowledge and to play the guardian of our cultural heritage would be endangered.

Research-supported higher education will unquestionably play a major role on our way towards the "knowledge society." The university will undoubtedly contribute to the change of society; however, by doing so, it will also have to transform itself. First, it has to become more flexible and more entrepreneurial. In spite of the importance of autonomy, it has to see itself as partner of the other constituents of society, e.g., industry and government. The university has to become aware of the scarcity of financial resources, thus setting priorities without jeopardizing its own creative potential. It is also important that the university accepts the fact that there will be other players, and that it can no longer expect to enjoy a kind of monopoly in research and higher education. Nevertheless, its competitive edge will always remain the research-driven education. From a managerial point of view, the future university needs leadership and participation, networking and focussing as well as a long-term output-oriented culture.

Looking at the university's mission, several major changes have to be envisaged. If the university intends to contribute to the development of society, it has to deal with and to anticipate major societal issues. It does not suffice to produce, maintain, and distribute knowledge; there are additional, equally important tasks. The very successful monodisciplinary, deterministic concept of research has apparently also created many problems, and is unable to answer many of the burning questions of a modern society. New concepts permitting the asking of new and differently structured questions have to be developed. New concepts must be developed in interdisciplinarity, system orientation, and contextual research and education. Such concepts and a general guiding principle, such as sustainable development, are new requirements that may well reshape higher education. Lifelong learning as well as the serious problem of how to reconcile an ever-rising number of students with the need for high quality and originality (i.e., mass university versus elite university) will become a major challenge. Finally, the ever-increasing complexity of society with its inherent nonpredictability, and the continuously growing power of humans to exploit and even destroy nature will have to be counteracted by a greater awareness of responsibility, accountability, and ethics. These ideas are certainly not new; the famous French writer, physician, and eminent humanist François Rabelais wrote in the sixteenth century that *"Science sans conscience n'est que ruine de l'âme"* ("Science without conscience is no more than ruin of the soul").

UNIVERSITY'S RESPONSE TO THE CHALLENGE OF THE NEW CENTURY

To fulfil its role as a future-oriented institution, the university must not only develop a vision and set goals and objectives, it must also transform itself. This transformation is a prerequisite for the accomplishment of its new mission. A whole array of key elements has to be taken into account.

- culture
- governance (structure, management, etc.)
- funding
- concepts of research, education, and services
- inter- and intra-university communication and relations
- selection criteria for admission of students
- planning and quality control (peer reviews, assessment of teaching, etc.)

Although the research-based European university will to a great extent remain a state university, it still has to adapt and change. European universities are rather conservative. Also, they traditionally lack a high degree of corporate identity. Autonomy and freedom are major traits. Even at the level of a single institution, the links between faculties representing different disciplines, and also between different chairs, are often weak. In continental Europe, the vice-chancellor or rector often has a purely representative role. The administration is often in the hands of civil servants, and the allocation of resources is determined by the public administration. To transform itself, the traditional process- or input-oriented university has to adapt to an output, result, and target-oriented culture—a major change indeed. The university is in search of leadership and a structure that allows for an output-orientation, and management keywords (e.g., allocation of competence and resources, delegation, etc.) often suddenly appear. The university's relationship with the political system and its position therein have to be rethought. There are, of course, risks and pitfalls. The cultural change might lead to a hierarchical structure with inherent risks, such as the dominance of a major decision maker, thus threatening the overall creative potential of the institution, or the so-called new public management might lead to a new, but equally inefficient, bureaucracy.

However, experience has shown that without a change in culture and governance, the university is not able to adapt to new needs arising from either society or science. Yet, the university always has to bear in mind that it is not identical with an industrial organization, and that its major targets remain society and human beings. Moreover, its constituency is enormously complex. Students cannot be considered exclusively as one of the most important "products" of the university. They are learning with the assistance of teachers; however, teachers are also learning from their students. This development shows the importance of a well-thought-out decision-making process. The new university's potential and success will heavily depend on its capability to take advantage of the creativity of all its members by means of an adequate participation and decision-sharing culture.

The university of tomorrow will impart to its students the highest standards of knowledge and practical skills. It will seek to enable young people to find their orientation in a complex and rapidly changing world, and to stimulate an understanding of ethical and cultural values so that, upon completion of their studies, they will not only be highly qualified professional people, but also responsible members of society.

The university will not be content with mere participation in solving already known problems. In the context of global civilization, it must respond to changing conditions and identify new problems as a kind of early warning system. It must also assume a leading role in seeking solutions. In doing so, it will depend on the spirit of discovery, the innovative force and flexibility of its members.

One of the major weaknesses of European universities lies in the transfer of knowledge and technology from the academic institution to its partners in industry and the economy. It is of paramount importance for Europe as a whole to remedy this situation. Therefore, a multitude of measures has to be taken, not only with regard to educational programs, but also concerning co-operation with industry. As a consequence, changes in governance, e.g., the establishment of a council or of ties with personalities from industry, the economy, and other important domains of society, have to be carried out, and sponsoring by industrial partners should no longer be considered as a threat to autonomy, but as a means of creating mutually beneficial interactions.

In conclusion, the European university's response to the challenge and the needs of the twenty-first century lies in its capability to transform itself. For many of the traditional institutions of research and higher education, the necessary change will have an impact on teaching, research, services, and governance. Even if the search for new knowledge, the search for a better understanding of ourselves, or the search for improved technical solutions continues, the threat to our very existence due to the spread of human civilization, as well as humankind's most urgent problems—poverty, hunger, diseases—demand that we find new approaches to knowledge and skills. It is my firm believe that a network of knowledge and skills acquired in an interdisciplinary environment best responds to the natural and cultural inter-dependencies of life. By integrating the natural sciences, technology, the humanities, and the social sciences, we can devise innovative concepts of education and research that will allow us to tackle the enormous challenges facing humankind, and that will help us blaze the way for a meaningful and sustainable development of present and future civilizations.

REFERENCES

Bush, V. (1945). *Science—The Endless Frontier.* Washington, D.C., Report to the President.
Drucker, P.F. (1993). *Post-Capitalist Society.* New York: HarperBusiness, p. 1.
Kennedy, P.M. (1994). *Preparing for the Twenty-First Century.* Fontana Press, special overseas edition.

CHAPTER 16

Future Challenges Facing American Higher Education

Chang-Lin Tien

The American system of higher education is very strong and much admired around the world, but it is confronting tremendous challenges as it moves into the next century, as are systems of higher education worldwide. Major global forces of change and social trends are transforming political, social, and educational institutions. Universities—traditionally among the most conservative of institutions in terms of institutional dynamics and change—must recognize these trends and be ready to respond constructively and creatively to these forces for change.

GLOBAL TRENDS IN A CHANGING WORLD

Described below are some of the most powerful forces for change in the modern world.

1. Perhaps the most fundamental force for change in the twentieth century is the spread of democracy and the free market. This trend toward democratization cannot be reversed, and it has many consequences. In a democracy, everyone has a voice, and everyone and his or her constituency want a piece of the pie. Facing increasing competition from various societal needs for financial resources and the need to provide higher education to the masses, academic institutions are seeing the breakdown of the traditional elitist educational structures and a trend away from the university as we have known it for centuries.

As countries enter the free market system, they become more competitive and focused on short-term goals. Short-term goals and pressing issues usually win out over long-term investments, to the ultimate detriment of higher education, which must plan for and exist for long-term goals. In a highly competitive environment, it is difficult for investment in higher education to get the same attention as such immediate, pressing, short-term issues as social welfare, public health, crime prevention, traffic congestion, and environmental remediation. It will take great leadership and visionary force to reverse this trend and maintain a proper level of investment in higher education.

In a democratic environment, universities must be more accountable, not only to the trustees or regents, but also to the students, the faculty, the nonacademic staff, the relevant federal and local government agencies, the general public, and the alumni. Each of these constituencies is expecting to see a prudent use of resources in general, but an increasing share for its own. Maintaining accountability to these constituencies without sacrificing long-term goals is a formidable balancing act and a tremendous challenge.

2. Rapid advances in information technology and telecommunications are also revolutionizing our daily lives, making the concept of a global village a reality; this revolution is, in turn, beginning to transform the university. New technologies provide opportunities to expand the range of services and outreach of the institutions and to explore and create new ways of delivering the essential product—knowledge. Leaders in higher education will have to encourage an openness and experimentation with these new technologies or be paralyzed in the constricted boundaries of tradition. Likewise, the tremendous revolution in biotechnology and life sciences will increasingly turn the research and teaching agenda toward greater emphasis on biomedical, environmental, and other quality-of-life issues.

3. Our communities, workplaces, and social institutions are becoming more diverse. Economic and financial systems are rapidly globalizing and becoming closely interconnected throughout the world. Universities must increasingly reflect the cultural and ethnic diversity of the global village we inhabit—in the campus environment, student enrollment, faculty, staff, and leadership. Internationalism and multiculturalism will be essential for the health of society and to the success of its academic institutions.

IMPACT ON AMERICAN HIGHER EDUCATION

All the following trends are having an effect on American schools as well.

1. We are seeing a tremendous expansion and diversification among colleges and universities in the United States, and this diversification is probably our greatest strength. Some people predict that in 10 or 20 years the number of universities in the U.S. will increase to 5,000 from the current number of about 3,000. We have large schools with more than 50,000 students on campus and small, equally famous and prestigious institutions like CalTech with only 1,800 students. We have public schools and private. We have specialized schools focused on engineering or science; we have small liberal arts colleges; we have religious schools and many new professional schools. The San Francisco Bay Area has at least 10 new, small universities, all serving different groups of students, such as the re-entry student. Overall, there is tremendous diversification and a spirit of experimentation not often found in other countries.

2. The steady decline in state and federal funding is a significant issue for institutions of higher education, whether public or private. Universities are competing for increasingly scarce public funds, competing even for the same students. Among established institutions, we are seeing an increasing bifurcation between the "haves" and the "have-nots," just as in society at large. The rich schools are becoming richer, the poor are becoming poorer. The best students are competing for admission to the same few top schools. An interesting example of this bifurcation is in the distribution of the National Science Foundation fellows among American research universities in the last few years. The NSF fellows as a group represent the best of the science and engineering college graduates going on to Ph.D. studies. Nearly 80 percent of the fellows are concentrated in four schools—Berkeley, Harvard, MIT, and Stanford.

3. Another outcome of the competition for resources is transformation of the "ivory tower" to a less autonomous or isolated enterprise. We see ever-increasing collaboration among universities, interdisciplinary programs within and between institutions, and close collaboration with private industry. These closer alliances between universities and industry can greatly benefit a university's research, but universities must be careful not to be unduly influenced by industry's wishes or sacrifice the university's autonomy in its scholarly pursuit. With budgets becoming tight, we need to look at effective ways of sharing academic resources, collaborating with other institutions, consolidating departments or even abolishing them, joint teaching, and shared teaching.

4. A changing workforce is also having an impact on American higher education in the proliferation of new, emerging institutions such as the University of Phoenix, a for-profit university mainly for continuing education, which is now the largest and fastest-growing university in the U.S. As knowledge is expanding, so is the need for lifelong learning. Professional schools, university extension courses, online instruction, and correspondence courses are all providing necessary responses to this growing need. Lifelong learning may be the norm for future generations of students, and systems of higher education will need to expand their outreach and services in support of it.

IMPACT ON RESEARCH UNIVERSITIES

Described below are major implications for research universities.

1. Students applying today to research universities like U.C. Berkeley are more competitive, diverse, and pragmatic than ever before. Competition for admission is intense. Last fall, Berkeley admitted 8,400 out of 27,000 students who applied for first-year admission, and actually registered about 3,600 new students. Most of the 27,000 applicants were already ranked among the top one-eighth of their graduate class.

    Berkeley's student body is often characterized by its diversity, wherein no one racial or ethnic group constitutes a majority. All age groups and economic, cultural, and geographic backgrounds are represented. This is a dynamic mix, producing the wide range of opinion and perspective essential to a great university. It has been said that by the year 2050, 60 to 70 percent of the workforce will be composed of people of color. If universities are not educating and preparing to educate a more diverse group of leaders and workers, they and society will face tremendous problems.

    Students who in the past would have chosen to pursue an academic career are now tending toward business or other professional majors, especially American-born students. It is alarming that fewer of our top talents want to make their full career in the academic area, and this trend has significant implications for future faculty and leadership in American universities.

2. Our faculty members are also changing. Today's professors are mobile and unlikely to spend their entire careers in one institution or to be involved over the long term in leadership within their university community. They are entrepreneurs, establishing their individual careers and reputations, courting outside funding, consulting with industry, and

collaborating with outside associations. Increasingly less is the "old fashioned" institutional loyalty and commitment.

3. In turn, academic departments, which constitute the most important and fundamental units in academia, are rapidly changing as well. The traditional departmental boundaries are weakening as more interdisciplinary programs and studies develop. Individual faculty members are becoming more externally active and connected and more internally assertive with self-interest. The department chairmanship is no longer a secure, powerful position required for strong, dynamic leadership.

4. Central administration has become increasingly complex as relationships between disciplines and institutions evolve, and we now see more professionals and fewer scholars serving in positions of university leadership. This trend may pose a great danger for the decision-making process in universities, where academic scholarship and learning should always remain as the highest goals.

5. At the same time, trustees or regents are becoming more assertive and politicized, sometimes asserting their right over traditional faculty prerogatives. Well-established administration–faculty shared governance relationships are often under attack.

6. The public and alumni are also actively engaging with universities and demanding a voice as well. While these engagements are generally essential and positive, they may also become unwelcome intrusions, especially in some university activities such as sports and industrial liaison.

CONCERNS AND OPPORTUNITIES

Described below are some major dangers and opportunities facing universities.

1. University administrators must retain a clear commitment to the academic mission, which is at the heart of every institution of higher education. At the same time, each institution must begin to define its own vision and selective focus. No one university can do everything it would like to do and maintain excellence at every level. Defining the university's vision is one of the most important issues facing higher education today. I see many universities flailing about, doing things without knowing exactly what they are doing or why. And administrators in general are not doing as good a job as they can. Reform is needed, based on long-term goals, purposes, and objectives.

2. We also have to look at the structure of university governance. U.C. Berkeley professors have always been number one in terms of faculty power in shared governance, although the regents have been challeng-

ing some of their powers. I believe that we need to review the entire system of relationships among faculty, students, university employees, and regents—all the structural issues. Heads of universities are accountable to many constituencies, and it is alarming that many top people don't want to seek university leadership any more, or burn out and rotate out of positions at an ever-increasing pace.

3. Financial management and control are issues of critical urgency. While American corporations have adjusted to meet the demands of the future by cutting costs and becoming more efficient, higher education has not caught up. We must begin to think in terms of portfolio management—taking the opportunity to enhance the university's resources rather than just reacting to declining and shifting resources.

4. Universities are not doing enough to embrace and to reap the benefits of the revolution in information technology (IT). I always believe in finding the opportunity in every crisis. The IT revolution will be a crisis only for those institutions that do not enthusiastically and creatively seize its possibilities for their own advantage.

5. Just as the workplace has changed radically, so will the classroom. We have to rethink the curriculum and the learning environment, looking at new ways to share knowledge, forge new alliances, and employ distance learning and shared teaching.

In summary, American educators need to face these concerns, initiate the required changes, and seize the opportunities presented or be left behind. Innovative long-term planning and visionary leadership are needed.

CHAPTER 17

The New University

Frank H. T. Rhodes

K nowledge has become the currency of the new global market; the most successful societies in the future will be those that optimize the creation, distribution, and utilization of knowledge. In this optimization, the universities will play a crucial role.

If our future well-being depends in some measure on the effectiveness of our research universities, what expectations should we have for these institutions? What should the best universities of the twenty-first century look like? Without pretending that anyone can provide a precise blueprint for the research university of the future, several characteristics seem essential. My description will be limited to the American university, not because I think it either the most important or the most likely to serve as a model for those in other places, but only because I know it best. The New American University will prosper to the extent that it can maintain a dynamic equilibrium between several inherent tensions.

CHARACTERISTICS OF THE NEW AMERICAN UNIVERSITY

Described below are what would appear to be some of the most likely and important characteristics of the New American University:

This article will form part of the concluding chapter in a forthcoming book.

1. Institutional autonomy, lively faculty independence and vigorous
   academic freedom, but strong, impartial, public governance and
   decisive, engaged presidential leadership

The American university has prospered, in part, because it has enjoyed an effective and responsive pattern of shared governance that has
served it well. Unlike some of its counterparts in other places, this shared
governance has typically involved a three-fold pattern of public oversight and trusteeship; shared, collegial internal governance by the faculty, and strong presidential leadership. Though the particulars have
varied with time and place, this three-fold pattern has proved both
durable and effective. Its effectiveness has depended in the past on a
large measure of external public confidence and internal institutional
loyalty, mutual trust, professional commitment, and impartial judgment.
However, these qualities, together with the pattern of shared governance they have supported, now show signs of strain.

Public governance, exercised by lay boards of trustees or regents,
remains strong, effective, and responsible in the private universities, but
highly variable in the public institutions, where board members are
typically appointed by the governor, or, in a few states, elected in state-
wide ballots. Political pressures, regional interests, ideological issues, and
obsessive notions of accountability have divided public boards, while
sunshine laws—ruthlessly applied—have limited their ability to recruit
outstanding and outspoken presidential leaders. Meanwhile, faculty
loyalty has tended to drift from the university to external professional
guilds, funding agencies, corporate sponsors, and private patrons, so that
institutional engagement of faculty members has often declined, or is
sometimes used to promote special interests or obstruct proposed reforms.

The role of the president—once an influential public figure and a
considerable external voice—is now seen by external observers as less
and less influential, and by potential aspirants as less and less desirable
and less and less effective, so that the average incumbency has declined
to less than five years in public institutions and less than seven in all
institutions.

As a result of these changes, institutions once admired as models of
prudent judgment and strong participatory government are now seen by
some as archetypes of bureaucratic bumbling and learned inefficiency,
where effective management and decisive leadership are held hostage to
a host of competing interests and divided loyalties and where prompt,
responsible action and responsive decisions are delayed by prolonged
debate or diluted by ideological wrangling. The development of responsible, effective, and balanced governance, leadership, and management

is one of the most urgent priorities for the American university as it contemplates the new millennium.

2. Increasingly privately supported, but increasingly publicly accountable and socially committed

Today's leading research universities include both privately endowed and state-supported, public institutions, though the financial differences between the two have declined in recent years as state appropriations have been reduced. One president of a public university has commented wryly that, within his own tenure, his university had changed from state-supported to state-assisted to state-located! As this trend continues, all major universities—public, as well as private—are likely to become more dependent on private support. Two campuses of the University of California, as well as the University of Michigan, for example, have each embarked on billion-dollar funding-raising campaigns. In 1995-96, voluntary giving to American universities and colleges reached $12 billion, increasing in 1996-97 to $13.8 billion, with some 53 percent coming from alumni and other individual donors. Of that total, research universities received $9.4 billion, with rather more than half of that going to public universities. Of the top 20 institutions in total giving, 8 were public.

Generally speaking, the private universities have been smaller in size, more selective in admissions, and more limited in range of academic programs than their public counterparts. But they have enjoyed more freedom—being unaffected, for example, by the requirement imposed on state universities to conduct virtually all their business in public—and more effective governance than most public institutions, where trustees or regents are politically appointed or elected. Against this, private universities have generally been far less engaged in community outreach and extension activities than have their public counterparts, largely because of the lack of funding for such efforts.

It seems likely that, as all universities become more dependent on private support, the New American University will see reforms in the governance of public institutions and greater emphasis by the private institutions on community outreach and service, with the land-grant extension model reinvented and reapplied on a new scale and in a new context. And both are likely to face a new level of public accountability, based not only on costs, but also on effectiveness.

3. Campus-rooted, but internationally oriented

In spite of the growing benefits of information technology, the New American University will still depend on an established campus base as the essential platform for both its specialized facilities and its scholarly community. Though its role may change, the traditional concept of a university as a place is unlikely to be made redundant by a virtual institution, however powerful and inclusive distance learning may become. But the "real" university, though it may be located in a particular place, cannot be confined to a single place; campus-based in its location, it will be international in its orientation and cosmopolitan in its character; its graduates will pursue their careers within an increasingly global economy and an increasingly diverse workforce. Both its curriculum and its membership will reflect this diversity; the underrepresented and the underserved will still be recruited; study abroad will become the norm; both the student and faculty bodies will become conspicuously international in their membership, and living productively in a diverse community will increasingly come to be regarded as a "job skill." International students already form a significant proportion of the university's student body (typically 10-15 percent of its undergraduates and up to 50 percent of its graduate students) and foreign-born faculty members are already found at all levels within the ranks of most of its departments. Boards of trustees of private universities already generally include several international members. New research partnerships, teaching exchanges, scholarly consortia, and institutional associations all serve to reinforce these growing international linkages. This emphasis on global knowledge is scarcely new; it recapitulates and reflects a characteristic as old as the university itself. While most colleges and universities will still draw their students from their local regions, the great research universities will become ever more international in their membership and outlook.

4. Academically independent, but constructively partnered

The New American University will continue to enjoy the remarkable degree of institutional independence and academic freedom that has marked its recent existence and been an essential part of its success. That scholarly independence—exasperating as it has sometimes been to its detractors, and buttressed, as needed from time to time by boards of trustees and courts of justice—has served society well.

The New American University and its scholarship will continue to depend on that *independence*, but it will thrive to the extent that it also acknowledges its own *dependence* on others. For no institution, however wealthy, can "do it all." No university, however large, can be truly comprehensive in its programs. Nor should it seek to be. If the university is to meet the increasing range of societal needs, it will require new alliances within the academic community and new partnerships outside it, with communities; local, state, and national agencies; corporations; foundations; hospitals; professional associations; scholarly societies; and other institutions—from other universities, schools, and colleges to federal research laboratories—to enrich and extend its scholarly work and support its services. Because the traditional "university-years" are but one part of a lifelong learning experience, universities will establish closer cooperation with other "providers" and "users" of knowledge, including not only other universities, professional associations, corporations, and local groups, but also commercial vendors of educational hardware and software.

5. **Knowledge-based, but student-centered; research-driven, but learning-focussed**

The distinctive feature of the New American University will still be its commitment to learning in its widest sense. This involves not simply the transmission of existing knowledge, but also the creativity that produces new achievements, and the research that leads to new discovery and new knowledge. World-class scholarship will require both greater selectivity and greater interaction among disciplines than is now the case. But this will be pursued in the context of a student-centered culture, with clear educational goals, explicit statements of curricular objectives, clearly defined professional skills, and new measures of educational outcome. It will include a new commitment to effective learning at every level—professional, graduate, and especially undergraduate—with emphasis on clearly defined standards, high competence, effective advising and mentoring, cultivation of learning skills, personal growth, individual creativity, and meaningful assessment, all based on a variety of learning styles, teamwork, off-campus experience, lifelong learning, and the effective use of educational technology.

The "best" universities and colleges of the future will be those demonstrating the most effective gains in learning and learning skills among their students. This new accountability will demand a better understanding of the learning process and a clearer statement of instructional purpose and effectiveness. The traditional pattern of a student accumulating information—however advanced—and a professor teaching "subjects"—however effectively—will be displaced by an emphasis on developing in students the initiative, skills, and discipline to pursue knowledge independently, to evaluate and weigh it effectively, and to apply it creatively and responsibly.

6. **Technologically sophisticated, but community-dependent**

Harnessing all the power of new information technology, both on the campus and in distance learning, the New American University will display a greater dependence on the power of the scholarly community in both teaching and research. The new electronic community will reinforce and complement the older resident community, each contributing the power of distributed intelligence in both inreach into the campus community and outreach beyond it. Intellectual cross-fertilization will become a more powerful learning tool and a more effective means of research and inquiry.

7. Quality-obsessed, but procedurally efficient

Because scholarly discipline and analytical rigor are the keys to understanding, the New American University will continue to be obsessed with quality. It can have no other standard. But scholarly quality and academic excellence are not inconsistent with administrative efficiency and cost-effectiveness. Universities have too readily assumed that, because quality is priceless, cost was no object, that no support level could ever be fully adequate for their needs. A new commitment to both excellence and cost-effectiveness, with thoughtful translation of quality improvement, effective practices, and meaningful benchmarking, will be applied across the campus.

For most universities, this task will have to be undertaken within a context of continuing financial constraint. Cost-effectiveness is likely to be a major factor in both student choice in enrollment and in corporate—and institutional—choice in creating new partnerships for "outsourcing" education and research. This will require continuous improvement in the effectiveness of the learning process, not so much in cost-cutting, as such, as in improving quality and performance. New and sophisticated measures of "output" and effectiveness will be required to satisfy public accountability.

8. Professionally attuned, but humanely informed

The growth in importance of professional studies has been paralleled by a decline in influence of the traditional liberal arts. This is partly cause and effect, influenced in part by the growing importance and increasing public role of the professions, and by the growing popularity of professional studies among students. But part of the decline in the influence of the liberal arts reflects the lack of internal cohesion within their own traditional core disciplines. The sciences have become powerful, but increasingly unintelligible to nonscientists. The social sciences, entranced by microanalysis and quantification, have become increasingly irrelevant to social issues and public policy. The humanities, embracing fragmentation, otherness, and unreality, have neglected the great overarching issues of human commonality in favor of partisan advocacy.

Yet never has professional practice stood in a greater need of enlightened influence and humane awareness. There is limited value and little benefit in information, undigested and unscrutinized by personal reflection, or in professional skills, unguided by thoughtful insight and personal commitment. If the university fails to educate free and responsible citizens, who will undertake the task? So the New American University must reinvent the liberal arts, perhaps expanding the range of cultural statement by the creative integration of sound, text, and image, and using the new communications technology to create both a new form of expression and a new level of literacy. This integration is, as yet, characterized more by trash than by pearls, more by entertainment than by enlightenment. But it offers the possibility of enriched cultural expression and a new cultural literacy to which the traditional liberal arts have yet to respond.

CONCLUSIONS

These eight characteristics seem likely to shape, and perhaps define, the New American University. They will change the culture of the campus, in much the same way that the changes of the late nineteenth century transformed the American college into the more comprehensive research university. The transformation will involve a combination of the best in the current model with the external connections and service ethic of the public land-grant university and with new global partnerships as strong as those of multinational corporations.

How creatively the university deals with these tensions will depend on the strength of its core values and its willingness to adapt to changing conditions and needs. This adaptation will involve changes—some of them wrenching—within the university. But American universities need to change, not because they are weak, but because they are strong. American universities are not "in trouble," not in decline. In spite of financial pressures, which are real, and public concerns, some of them justified, universities are doing well. They include world-class institutions; a dozen or so provide the benchmark for the rest of the world.

So change for the sake of change offers no benefits. But responsive and responsible change is the requirement for their continuing strength, and their continuing effectiveness. Like it or not, universities were originally created and continue to enjoy public support because they are "service organizations," serving the growing needs of society for knowledge and professional skills and service. But that responsibility is best discharged not by immersion in the issues of the moment, but by taking the larger, comprehensive view of knowledge, in all its dimensions. The community that is a university is the best means yet devised for achieving that comprehensive view, with all its benefits. Perhaps the biggest challenge for the university is to balance the inevitable tension between that scholarly community, and the degree of separation that sustains it, and responsible concern for the clamoring needs of society.

University trustees, deans, provosts, and, especially, presidents must become the challengers of complacency, the voices of institutional conscience, the patient advocates for change, the champions of excellence, the midwives of new alliances and partnerships, the facilitators of teamwork, and the untiring exemplars of both traditional values and a new level of commitment.

In an age of limits and constraints, of cynicism and suspicion, universities must reaffirm the soaring possibilities that enlightened education represents. In an era of broken families, dwindling religious congregations, decaying communities, our nation desperately needs a new model of community—knowledgeable but compassionate, critical but concerned, skeptical but affirming—that will serve the clamoring needs of our fragmented society and respond to the nobler, unuttered aspirations of our deeper selves.

This is not to pretend that universities have either wholesale solutions to humanity's ills or a monopoly on skills to address them. Universities are human creations, full of human imperfection, with as much sloth, envy, malice, and neglect as any other community and rather more than their share of pettiness, arrogance, and pride. But it is to assert that universities, with all their imperfections, represent the crucible within which our future will be formed. Boiling, steaming, frothing at times, a new amalgam must somehow be created within them if we are to surmount our social problems and rediscover the civic virtues on which our society depends. And, as leaders in every field of endeavor are educated within their walls, as knowledge is increased within their laboratories, new works created within their studios, and professional practice developed and refined within their facilities, so universities provide each new generation of leaders, educated, influenced, and shaped within the culture of the campus. This emerging community—analytical and affirming, critical and creative, inclusive and inquiring, engaged and enabling—will be the New American University.

APPENDIX

•••••••••••••

The Glion Declaration

APPENDIX

The Glion Declaration
The University at the Millennium

The new millennium, into which we move and which our children will inherit, confronts us with a bewildering mixture of promise and threat. On the one hand, we glimpse the promise of revolutionary advances in biomedicine, communications, information technology, alternative energy sources, new materials, automation and globalization; on the other hand, we contemplate the looming threats of balkanization, tribalism, terrorism, sectarianism, north-south inequalities, hunger, the intricate balance between population, resources and environment, the challenge of sustainable development and the relationship of all these to the future of traditional nation-states. And, if the balance between promise and threat is unclear, what *is* clear is that the essential key—though not the only key—to human well-being in this daunting new world is knowledge.

Between May 13 and 17, 1998, a group of 10 Western Europeans and 10 Americans, all of whom were long closely associated with higher education, met in Glion, Switzerland, to discuss the challenges facing the higher education systems in their countries in the new millennium. Besides examining these challenges in depth, the Glion Colloquium participants proposed promising new initiatives to meet the challenges. At the request of his fellow members of the Glion Colloquium, Professor Frank H.T. Rhodes, president emeritus of Cornell University, gave expression to the collective views of the participants in the form of the Declaration reprinted here. The Declaration was previously published in English and in French as "The Glion Declaration: The University at the Millennium." Geneva: The Glion Colloquium, 1998, 9p., and in the Fall 1998 issue of *The Presidency*, pp. 26–31.

Now knowledge is not a free-good; it is not a naturally-occurring resource. It is a personal discovery, an individual creation. It comes only to the prepared mind, coaxed into existence by personal reflection and inquiry, individual discovery, sophisticated research and costly exploration. And it can be received, understood, and applied only by the educated and informed individual. Those things on which the future of humankind will chiefly depend in the new millennium—education, personal skills, natural resources, effective capacities, sustainable communities, as well as wise leadership, informed choice, national discipline, sound policies, international agreements, the humane use of technology and the judicious and benevolent use of resources—will depend increasingly on knowledge: knowledge discovered, knowledge gained, knowledge tested, knowledge shared, knowledge applied. And these things, in turn, will require wisdom: the way in which knowledge is weighed and used.

Knowledge is the core-business of the university. In every aspect of its discovery, testing, dissemination and application, the universities of the world play a crucial role. In this role, they are not alone. They are part of a great network of tertiary education; they depend on the work of schools and colleges; they are partners with professional associations, non-government organizations, industry, business, research institutes, hospitals, government agencies and international organizations; they share the concerns and contribute to the needs of their communities, regions and nations. But, beyond all these alliances and dependencies, vital as they are, the universities play a unique and crucial role. They are the chief agents of discovery, the major providers of basic research that underlies new technology and improved health care, they are the engines of economic growth, the custodians and transmitters of cultural heritage, the mentors of each new generation of entrants into every profession, the accreditors of competency and skills, the agents of personal understanding and societal transformation. In them, on a daily basis, the young and the old seek to bring wisdom, insight and skills to bear in the daunting complexities of human affairs.

The university is one of the greatest inventions of the present millennium: although created more than nine centuries ago, it remains one of the glories of human aspiration and one of the triumphs of the power of imagination. We, as members of its community of learning, challenge it to play a transforming role in society, and thus to transform itself.

TO THE UNIVERSITY: A CALL TO IMAGINATIVE BOLDNESS AND RESPONSIBLE FREEDOM

Universities are learning communities, created and supported because of the need of students to learn, the benefit to scholars of intellectual community, and the importance to society of new knowledge, educated leaders, informed citizens, expert professional skills and training, and individual certification and accreditation. Those functions remain distinctive, essential contributions to society; they form the basis of an unwritten social compact, by which, in exchange for the effective and responsible provision of those services, the public supports the university, contributes to its finance, accepts its professional judgment and scholarly certification, and grants it a unique degree of institutional autonomy and scholarly freedom. Within this compact, the university has a reciprocal obligation for impartial scholarship, the highest professional competence and integrity, the cultivation of advanced knowledge and a love of learning among its students, and a sensitivity towards the need for its services in society at large.

The situation confronting all nations—both industrialized and developing—now requires, as never before, an informed citizenry, an educated workforce, skilled in handling changing and increasingly sophisticated tasks, and this, in turn, requires not only achieving an optimum level in student enrollment, but also the means of providing and pursuing life-long learning. At the very time of these new demands, the universities are experiencing severe financial constraints, with increasing competition for scarce public funds for other pressing public needs. Yet these other social needs demand, in turn, a renewed public investment in higher education, as the need increases for creative solutions to social problems, sustainable development and the expansion of skilled professional services. Wise political leadership will be required to sustain long-term investment in learning, without which social advancement is an empty dream.

We call on our colleagues in the universities to recognize their unique responsibilities and opportunities to their communities, regions and the larger global society by:

Their affirmation that teaching is a moral vocation, involving not just the transfer of technical information, however sophisticated, but also the balanced development of the whole person. That will mean an emphasis on the development of a creative learning environment—rather than relying solely on the traditional pattern of formal lecturing and "one-way" teaching—the cultivation of a student-centered and student-friendly atmosphere and the goal of producing not only highly skilled, but also broadly educated, self-motivated graduates, with a thirst for life-long learning, aware of their heritage, conscious of their civic obligations and ethically responsible in their professional careers.

Their affirmation that scholarship is a public trust. All members of the university community—young and old—are committed to learning, and to the discovery and exploration on which it is based. Scholarship, though it is rooted in individual insight and personal inquiry, is a cooperative venture, supported by public funds and private patrons as a social enterprise, because it enriches human understanding and contributes to human well-being. That public support presupposes the impartiality and independence of the scholar, and the integrity of the scholarship. Two opportunities—new alliances and the use of information technology—now offer the possibility of expanding the range and usefulness of scholarship and providing unprecedented benefits to society.

Creating new intellectual alliances within the university and new partnerships outside it. Traditional disciplines, with their deliberate concentration and abstraction, are powerful engines of scholarship but, for all their power, they impose self-created canons and constraints on broader inquiry. Strong departments, for all their benefits, may restrict the range and limit the scope of critical investigation. Strong disciplinary expertise will continue to be essential, but, wedded to the insights and skills of those from other disciplines and professions, it now offers unusual promise in confronting broader public issues.

Partnership with institutions, agencies and corporations beyond the campus can supplement and extend the skills of the academy. Scholars have been slow to apply their skills to pressing social issues, partly, one supposes, because of their complexity and intransigence; partly, perhaps, because of a lack of both means and incentives to address them, and partly because the issues are often controversial and the risks of failure are high. But society needs the insight and expertise of the academy in all areas of great public concern. New alliances, new support and new incentives are needed to address them, just as the land grant university was created in response to the needs of mid-nineteenth-century America. These new alliances will not replace the norms and canons of traditional disciplines, but will be a powerful supplement to them.

Employing new information technology (IT), which now allows the organization of these partnerships on a grand scale, whether locally-focussed, or globally-based. This new technology can now provide massive interdisciplinarity, and experiment and simulation of undreamed-of power. It is likely to transform every aspect of the university's activities, but if its capacities are to be fully employed in their learning, research and public service, universities will need to encourage flexibility, entrepreneurism, experiment and breadth within their organizational structures and among all their members.

Recognizing public service as a major institutional obligation and providing the means and the incentives to pursue it. For all its independence and autonomy, essential as these are, the university has a social responsibility and a public obligation. It must use its autonomy, not as an excuse for isolation, indifference or advocacy, but as a means of making an independent contribution to society, providing an impartial voice and professional service to the public good.

Providing new structures, flexible career paths and selective support for new patterns of creative inquiry, effective learning, and responsible public service. Universities have proved remarkably adaptive over the centuries in responding to new challenges and novel opportunities. Financial constraint will, however, require the future development of new initiatives more by substitution, than by addition; this will strain existing hierarchies and structures, require new patterns of appointment and employment and demand new methods of funding and support. Antiquated structures, cumbersome procedures and narrow, exclusive career tracks are likely to require substantial modification if universities are to make the most effective contribution to changing challenges and opportunities.

Developing new patterns of governance, leadership and management that promote effective learning, creative scholarship and responsible service. Universities have prospered to the extent that they have developed an effective and responsive pattern of shared governance, which has served them well. This has typically involved a three-fold pattern of public oversight and trusteeship, shared collegial internal governance and informed—and generally consensual but often short-term—administrative leadership. Though the particulars have varied with time and place, this overall three-fold pattern has proved both durable and effective, but it now shows signs of intense strain. Some public governing boards have become more politicized than has been historically true, asserting authority over areas once viewed as faculty prerogatives; government ministries and state agencies in some countries have engaged in micro-management of university affairs; faculty councils have sometimes used their powers to promote special interests, delay action, and prevent proposed reforms; administrative leadership has been seen as too weak in some institutions and unwisely assertive in others, while effective management is widely seen as the casualty of these competing interests, held hostage to indecision, compromise and overlapping jurisdiction. At its best, the contemporary university is seen as a model of effective participatory governance; at its worst, it is seen as an archetype of bureaucratic bumbling and learned inefficiency.

All universities need to work with their stakeholders to ensure the preservation of the benefits of collegial governance and openness with the achievement of excellence, responsiveness and effectiveness in all their various activities. This will require institutions to clarify and redefine jurisdiction and responsibility; it may also require rethinking and strengthening the role of the rector/chancellor/president and the terms of appointment to this office.

Accepting the obligation for accountability. It is the public, through direct state and federal payments, tax exemption, voluntary support, corporate contributions and private gifts—as well as fees for service—such as student tuition, housing charges and patient fees, for example—who sustain the university. To them, the university must be openly and appropriately accountable for the prudent use of its resources. This accountability requires, of course, the fullest level of professional financial reporting and independent professional auditing. What it does not mean, however, is accommodation to every political pressure, popular-demand, public interest, scholarly fashion or social whim, whether from within or without. The university must be properly accountable for its "output"; the integrity of its scholarship, the quality of its professional standards, the impartiality of its judgments and the competence of its graduates. But, beyond those things, it must remain sturdily independent, yielding neither to internal activist interests, nor to external pressure, but changing deliberately, selectively and responsibly, in the light of public needs and changing knowledge. Anything less would make it truly unaccountable, as well as fundamentally compromising its essential function

Affirming the ancient values upon which the academy is established. In a society of shifting goals and uncertain values, the university must stand for something more than accurate data and reliable information; more, even than useful knowledge and dependable standards. The university is the custodian, not only of knowledge, but also of the values on which that knowledge depends; not only of professional skills, but of the ethical obligations that underlie those professional skills; not only of scholarly inquiry, disciplined learning and broad understanding, but also of the means that make inquiry, learning and understanding possible. In its institutional life and its professional activities, the university must reaffirm that integrity is the requirement, excellence the standard, rationality the means, community the context, civility the attitude, openness the relationship and responsibility the obligation upon which its own existence and knowledge itself depend.

For 900 years of the present millennium, the university, as a community dedicated to those values, has served society well. Its effectiveness in the new millennium will depend on its reaffirmation of those ancient values as it responds creatively to the new challenges and opportunities that confront it. This is the moment for both society and the university to reaffirm the social compact, on which the future of all our peoples will so largely depend, and for their leaders to work together towards the achievement of their common goals.

INDEX

by Linda Webster

United States universities *(cont.)*
  expansion and diversification
      among, 163
  as full-service organizations, 45
  funding for, 21–22, 37–38, 40–
      41, 65–67, 82
  future of, 43–50, 161–74
  governmental attitudes toward,
      22–23
  historical development of, 18, 48
  information technology and, 56–
      63
  learning culture future scenario
      of, 39, 48–50
  learning preferences of students
      in, 24
  libraries of, 129–33
  lifelong learning and, 136
  market-driven future scenario
      for, 39, 43–47
  media attitudes toward, 38
  mergers, acquisitions, and hostile
      takeovers of, 46–47
  New American University, 167–
      74
  number of, 46, 163
  policy issues facing, 52–53
  private universities, 15, 66, 67,
      68
  questions on, 52–53
  role of research university, 53
  societal needs for, 41
  structural inefficiencies in, 23
  student expectations of, 23–24
  survival and drop-out rates in,
      148
  survival or demise of, 4, 38, 40,
      52, 56–57, 66
  unbundling of, 45, 59
  work-based learning in, 143
Universities. *See also* Collaboration;
    European universities; Finance;

Governance; Research;
    Students; Teaching; United
    States universities; and specific
    universities
  access to, 8–9, 47, 61, 65, 71
  action agenda for, 53–54
  activist approach to change in,
      vii–viii, 4, 17, 25, 50–52, 66,
      173–74
  challenges of generally, viii–ix,
      3–20, 24–25, 39–44, 54–55,
      119, 156–66, 173–74
  changing environment and
      shape of, 4–7, 39–43
  comparison of institutions in
      United States and Western
      Europe, 15–16
  competitors of, 8, 13
  as conservative institutions, 4
  demand for higher education,
      41, 45, 56, 65, 66–67, 112,
      119
  "deregulation" of, 44, 46–47
  distinction between other
      educational institutions and,
      8
  enrollment statistics, 41, 45, 56,
      60, 67, 112, 120, 136–38,
      144, 164
  evolutionary path of change in,
      vii, 4, 17, 50–52, 56
  forces driving change in, 39–44,
      50–52
  four-sector new organization of,
      109–10
  future of, ix, 43–50, 155–60,
      158–60, 161–74, 177–82
  Glion Declaration on, 177–82
  globalization and, 5
  historical development of, 18,
      25, 26–28, 48, 56, 99